普通高等教育"十二五"高职高专规划教材

Practical English Writing

新编实用英语

写作（上册）

主　编	肖付良　高　平　刘　燕
副主编	陈海燕　苏燕飞　李嘉萱
编　委	（以姓氏笔画为序）
	史小平　刘美玲　刘　洋　彭晓颖

中国人民大学出版社

·北京·

图书在版编目（CIP）数据

新编实用英语写作. 上册 / 肖付良，高平，刘燕主编.—北京：中国人民大学出版社，2013.4
普通高等教育"十二五"高职高专规划教材
ISBN 978-7-300-17311-5

Ⅰ.①新… Ⅱ.①肖… ②高… ③刘… Ⅲ.英语–写作–高等职业教育–教材 Ⅳ.①H315

中国版本图书馆 CIP 数据核字（2013）第064553号

普通高等教育"十二五"高职高专规划教材

新编实用英语写作（上册）

主　　编　肖付良　高　平　刘　燕
副主编　陈海燕　苏燕飞　李嘉萱
编　　委　史小平　刘美玲　刘　洋　彭晓颖
Xinbian Shiyong Yingyu Xiezuo (Shang Ce)

出版发行	中国人民大学出版社	
社　　址	北京中关村大街31号	**邮政编码**　100080
电　　话	010-62511242（总编室）	010-62511398（质管部）
	010-82501766（邮购部）	010-62514148（门市部）
	010-62515195（发行公司）	010-62515275（盗版举报）
网　　址	http:// www. crup. com. cn	
	http:// www. ttrnet. com（人大教研网）	
经　　销	新华书店	
印　　刷	北京中印联印务有限公司	
规　　格	185 mm×260 mm　16开本	**版　　次**　2013 年 4 月第 1 版
印　　张	10.75	**印　　次**　2013 年 4 月第 1 次印刷
字　　数	230 000	**定　　价**　28.00 元

前 言
Preface

本教材以一名高职院校毕业生应聘涉外文员、涉外商务助理岗位，直至成长为外贸业务员等涉外商务从业人员的工作过程为主线，以其职业成长过程中工作所需的典型工作任务为主要内容，以培养涉外商务岗位就业所需的职业能力为目的进行编写。包括《新编实用英语写作（上册）》、《新编实用英语写作（下册）》两册。

本书为《新编实用英语写作（上册）》，共需约64学时。

一、编写原则

1. 创新性原则

以"工作过程导向"为设计理念，教学内容与涉外商务岗位的主要工作过程始终紧密相连，注重涉外商务岗位实际所需的综合职业能力的培养，消除大部分传统写作教材偏重知识体系的弊端，设计理念创新。

2. 职业性原则

广泛调研涉外商务行业，解构职业岗位，选取、整合、序化涉外商务岗位真实工作过程中的典型工作任务。一项典型工作任务为一个主题单元，每个单元又包括若干微工作任务。学习任务与工作任务有机融合，注重职业性。

3. 实用性原则

选择涉外商务活动中的真实语料作为教学材料，营造真实的语境，既有利于提高英语写作水平，又有利于培养涉外商务职业素质，针对性、实用性强。

4. 多维性原则

本教材配备教师用书、教学课件及网络资源，提供合理的教学建议及丰富的辅助资源，方便教师备课与授课，教学资源多维度。

二、教材特色

1. 教学理念注重创新

本教材以"工作过程导向"的教育理念为指导，将教学内容及教学过程与岗位工作过程紧密联系、商务英语写作学习与涉外商务岗位职业素质培养有机融合，从而提高英语写作技能及涉外商务职业素质，达到零距离就业的目的，真正体现职业性与应用性。

2. 教学设计注重职业

本教材在广泛调研涉外行业、企业的基础上确定编写方案，根据涉外商务岗位职业能力的要求，选取真实工作过程中的典型工作任务，并将其整合、序化为教学内容。设计主题单元，每单元为一项典型工作任务，每项任务又分为若干微工作任务。学习任务与工作任务有机融合，实现"教、学、做"一体化。

3、选材内容注重实用

本教材选择涉外商务活动中实际应用的真实语料作为教学材料，注重时代性与实用性。真实工作中的选材，能为学生营造真实的语境；学习内容与未来工作内容有机融合，能有效激发学生的学习兴趣。

4、教学资源注重多维

本教材根据教学需要，配备教师用书、教学课件、网络资源，提供合理的教学建议与丰富的辅助资源，以多维度的教学资源库方便教师备课与授课。

三、教学内容

本教材主要以从事涉外商务工作的人员进行日常商务文书写作所涉及的典型工作任务为框架，包括求职应聘、商务交际、办公室事务处理3项典型工作任务；每项典型工作任务由不同的微任务组成，这些微任务又共同组成一个完整的微工作过程。具体分为3个主题单元，共15课，即：求职应聘（商务写作综述、招聘启事、履历表、求职信）；商务交际（邀请信、感谢信、祝贺信、投诉信、道歉信）；办公室事务处理（通知、电子邮件、备忘录、会议纪要、商务报告、商业广告）。其中一个主题单元即一项典型工作任务，一课即一项微工作任务，每课分为6个模块。各模块由易到难、循序渐进、环环相扣，将典型工作任务与学习任务有机融合，让学生完成与工作任务紧密结合的学习任务，切实提高日常商务文书写作技能和涉外商务职业能力。

模块一　Objectives

明确每课所要掌握的总学习目标，主要包括知识目标、技能目标及语法目标。

模块二　Cultural Tips

介绍每课主题写作的相关知识，让学生了解其构成要素、写作要点和写作技巧等。

模块三　Warm-up Activities

通过图片展示、小组讨论、回答问题、表达看法等多种形式完成与主题单元相关的任务，激发学生对主题单元学习的兴趣，构架联系新旧知识的桥梁，达到激活学生思维、活跃课堂气氛的目的。

模块四　Sample Study

包括 Sample、Vocabulary、Notes、Expressions 等内容，通过典型样例学习，提炼完成主题单元微工作任务所需的主要词汇、表达法、写作格式与技巧等，掌握主题写作的相关知识及技能。

模块五　Practical Writing

根据与课文主题相关的工作任务设计练习，由 Sample Consolidation、Grammar Focus、Language Points、Letter Practice 构成。Sample Consolidation 主要通过填空、选择等练习，巩固样例所学知识。Grammar Focus 通过学习日常商务文书写作中使用频率高的语法规则，学会运用所学语法。Language Points 通过搭配词义、完成句子、翻译、选词填空等多种练习，熟练掌握主题单元写作所用的主要相关词汇、表达法。Letter Practice

通过完成短文、翻译、情景拟写等练习，熟练拟写格式规范、内容准确的日常商务信件。

模块六　Supplementary Reading

本部分遴选紧扣单元主题的补充阅读材料，是课内学习的延展及有益补充。

四、编写队伍

本册各编委为来自湖南娄底职业技术学院、内蒙古河套学院、湖南信息职业技术学院、湘潭职业技术学院等多所高等院校教学经验丰富的一线专业教师，主编为肖付良、高平、刘燕。肖付良负责全书的总纂、终审，副主编为陈海燕、苏燕飞、李嘉萱，参与编写的其他编委包括史小平、刘洋、刘美玲和彭晓颖。外籍专家 Ramon Battershall 先生也参与了本册的审稿工作。调研及编写过程中，得到了诸多行业专家、学者的帮助，在此深表感谢。

鉴于编者水平有限，疏漏在所难免，诚请各位使用者对教材的不足之处提出宝贵意见 (ldxfl@126.com)，以便我们今后修正完善。

编者

2013 年 1 月

目 录
Contents

Unit 1

Employment Correspondence
求职应聘

An Overview of Business Writing

Objectives

To be proficient in
◎ the useful words and expressions used in this lesson
◎ the definition of writing
◎ functions, types, principles and formats of business writing
◎ key elements of a business letter

Cultural Tips

A business letter is often written in formal language, and it usually can be used to request direct information or action from another party, to reply directly to a request, to apologize for a mistake, or simply to convey goodwill between organizations and their customers, clients and other external parties.

Part I
Warm-up Activities

◆ **Work in pairs and tick the key elements included in a complete business letter.**

Letterhead	(	)
Date	(	)
Attention line	(	)
Mailing notation	(	)
Body	(	)
References	(	)

What are the key elements?

3

Complimentary close	( )
Carbon copy	( )
Signature	( )
Inside address	( )

◆ **Work in pairs and write down the 5 Cs often used in business writing.**

_____

_____

_____

_____

Part II
An Overview of Business Writing

○ Introduction

With the increase of economic globalization and networking, the flow of information between minds is becoming more and more important. In business communication, a timely message may create a handsome profit or reduce huge losses. Therefore, as a means of communication, business writing is greeting a new era.

○ Definition of Writing

Before taking the course, you need first make yourself *acquainted* with what writing is. According to one of the *definitions* given by Collins-English Dictionary, writing refers to a group of letters or symbols written or *marked* on a surface as a means of communicating ideas by making each symbol stand for an idea, concept, or thing. Though we have other non-verbal ways of communicating, such as body language, speaking and writing with the characteristic of *involving* words has long been the two major communicative forms. Compared to speaking, writing has its advantages. One cannot produce a successful essay without careful thinking and close-knit organization. Moreover, pens as writing tools have already made a great contribution to keeping a permanent record of various human activities. With the further development of information technology, writing has broader ways. One can write an instant message in his mobile phone or personal computer even during a meeting where one is not allowed to speak, but everything will be OK when written. Therefore, writing is not less important than speaking from the point of view of communicative power.

O Functions of Business Writing

People write for different purposes, on which writing *classification* is based. A graduate writes an academic paper for his/her diploma; a scientist writes a lab report for his/her study; a businessman writes a market report for his business, etc. Therefore, business writing is about achieving business purposes, which involve both internal communication within the company and external communication; interfacing with the public or other organizations on behalf of the company. Generally business letters should have three functions—to inform, to persuade and to entertain.

O Common Types of Business Documents

With the widespread use of the internet, writing is even more involved in every part of business. It appears in letters, e-mails, memos, minutes, notices, reports, *proposals*, etc. Among these, letters, memos, e-mails and reports are generally considered the most *fundamental* types of business documents according to their frequency and characteristics in business practices.

Samples of Letters, Memos, E-mails and Reports

Letter

New World Toy CO., LTD.
No.36 Maizidian Street, Chaoyang District, Beijing — **Letterhead**
Tel.: 010-13632212 Fax: 010-1363221

May 20, 2011 — **Date**

Song Na
16 College Way — **Inside Address**
Oregon City, OR 26768

Dear Ms. Song, — **Salutation**

I wish to acknowledge receipt of your order for 30,000 pieces of plastic toy portable phones. I've already sent my assistant, Yuhua Su, to deal with your order and she will give you a reply — **Body** as soon as everything is arranged.
I shall look forward to doing further business with you.

Yours Sincerely, — **Complimentary Close**

Zhao Yi — **Signature**

Memo

To: All Department Deans — **Recipients Name and Job Title**
From: Xuhong Yang, Human Resource Manager — **Sender's Name and Job Title**
Date: 28 March, 2011 — **Completion Date**
Subject: In-service English Training — **Information Summary**

An English class will take place in the Training Centre.
Please encourage your own staff to attend the course.
Please send me the names of all interested staff by 9 a.m. on 1st April.

E-mail

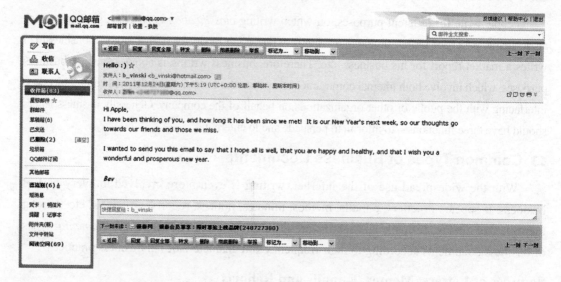

Report

stating briefly what the report is about

Report on Satisfaction with Employee Benefits

Terms of Reference —— explaining who wants the report and when it is submitted

Mr. Deqiang Wang, Director of Personnel, has requested this report on satisfaction with employee benefits. The report is to be submitted to him by Dec. 30th.

Procedure —— explaining how the information is collected and what it's mainly concerned about

A representative selection of 20% of the staff were interviewed in the period between Nov. 10th and Nov. 25th concerning:

◇ Overall satisfaction with our current benefits package

◇ Suggestions for the improvement of communication policies

◇ Problems encountered when dealing with our HMO (Health Maintenance Organizations)

Findings —— summarizing facts and ideas

◇ Employees are generally satisfied with the current benefits package, but they requested that their classroom payments should be increased.

◇ The most common suggestion for improvement is processing benefits requests online.

◇ Most teachers complained about the lack of insurance of occupational diseases in our benefits package.

Conclusions —— state facts and ideas

◇ The classroom payment should be increased.

◇ Our benefits request system should include the employee health insurance.

Recommendations —— putting forward suggestions for the actions to be taken based on findings

◇ The classroom payment should be increased to ¥50.

◇ Meet HMO representatives to discuss the complaints concerning the occupational disease insurance.

Xiaoyan Fang —— the writer's name and title

Assistant Director

◑ Principles of Effective Business Writing

What does a successful business letter look like? When the receiver interprets the sender's intention and the sender achieves his or her purpose, the writing is considered to be an effective one. So from the writer's point of view, it's advisable to follow the five Cs, namely, *clarity*, *correctness*, *conciseness*, *completeness* and *courtesy*.

1. Clarity

Clarity is regarded as the most important factor in written communication. The sender needs to tell the reader exactly what he or she should know by using the right word in the right place to make their purpose easily understood while reading. Therefore, you'd better use simple but correct words and short sentences instead of difficult and complex ones. Be careful to convey clear messages. You know, no message is much better than an incorrect one.

2. Correctness

On one hand, correctness means no mistakes in spelling, *punctuation*, grammar, and format. The writer should be concerned about the conventions of standard written English—to proofread to make sure that spelling is correct, grammar is *conventional*, punctuation aids in making sense, and that the format is acceptable. On the other hand, it means correct data, accurate  statements and clear opinions. These are the basic requirements of an effective business letter.

3. Conciseness

Conciseness is key to good business writing. A wordsmith writes in the strongest words, but not necessarily the fewest to achieve the goal. However, a successful business letter absolutely avoids unnecessary repetition and wordy statements, for businessmen would prefer to spend their time and patience on how to maximize the profits rather than reading long letters.

4. Completeness

All the necessary data and information should be included in a letter to provide the reader with sufficient details. An incomplete letter will resemble an incomplete song, leaving the audience an only wild guess, which could prove costly in certain situations. As one of the key components of successful business writing, completeness is expressed in every aspect of the letter.

5. Courtesy

The sender should pay special attention to the courtesy of business communication, which means treating people in a courteous and friendly tone. An effective writer should take into consideration the reader's desires, problems, circumstances, and possible responses to their request. To be courteous, the writer should avoid expressions that are likely to cause offense, but *concentrate* on what the reader is thinking about, and focus on the information of "you" instead of "I" or "we".

○ Elements of a Business Letter

A typical and professional-looking business letter usually includes the following eight elements: letter head, date, inside address, *salutation*, letter body, *complimentary* close, signature and enclosure.

1. Letterhead

The letterhead contains the writer's company name, address, telephone and fax number, and e-mail address. A logo or an emblem of the company is often contained in it. Sometimes extra information such as a telephone and fax number, e-mail address, website, etc. is listed after the address and before the date. But if the return address isn't imprinted on the *stationery*, it's necessary to type it.

2. Date

The date tells you when the writer writes the letter. There is a line's space between the date and the last line of the letterhead. The common typical formats are shown in American style (Month/Day/Year) or British style (Day/Month/Year). The full written form of the month is commonly preferred, in case abbreviation may cause confusion. The date position depends on the style you choose. It may appear on the left or right margin between the address and salutation.

3. Inside Address

In general, the inside address contains the addressee's complete title and name, which help the *recipient* route the letter properly if the address on the envelope is unreadable. Between the heading and the inside address, there is single spacing, and another line between the inside address and the salutation.

4. Salutation

The salutation is also known as a greeting, namely, it is used to greet the addressee. The conventional greeting is *Dear Sir(s)*, *Dear Madam/Mesdames*, or *Dear Mr./Ms.* with last name, with a subsequent comma or colon. If the letter is addressed to an individual, it's courteous to use the person's title and last name in the salutation, for example, *Dear Mr. Smith* rather than his full name, *Dear Mr. George Smith*. *Dear Sir or Madam,* and *Whom It May Concern* can be used when the sender doesn't know who will receive the letter, however, the latter is considered somewhat out of date.

5. Body

The body usually begins with two lines below the salutation that contains the message the sender wants his addressee to know. It's the most important part of a business letter. When you start to deal with this part, bear the 5 Cs in your mind. Take time to organize your thoughts and make sure that everything has been taken into consideration before you post it. Never underestimate the importance of the format. As the Chinese saying goes, *a good horse with a good saddle*, an appropriate format will make the receiver greatly impressed by your sincerity and good service. Be sure to single-space within the paragraph but double-space between paragraphs.

6. Complimentary Close

The complimentary close brings a letter to a close in a polite way. Conventionally, "Truly yours" or "Yours truly" are for unknown addressees, and "Sincerely yours", or "Yours sincerely" for known ones. According to the letter style, it can be either placed at the left margin, or you can set its left edge in the center of the letter sheet.

7. Signature

The signature consists of two parts. One is the writer's handwritten name, the other is the typed name. For the sake of recognition, the typed name comes three to four lines below complimentary close, sometimes titles as well. Between them is the handwritten name that is signed in ink instead of with a rubber stamp, because signing with a rubber stamp is regarded as a form of *discourtesy*. Women may place "Miss", "Mrs.", "Ms." or similar titles in brackets before their names to announce how they wish to be addressed.

8. Enclosure (or Attachment)

Just as its name implies, "enclosure" means an additional document that is enclosed in the letter. When sending an *enclosure* in a business letter, the writer should place the abbreviations (Enc., or Encl.) of Enclosure or write the word "Enclosure" at the bottom of the letter on the left-hand side. This reminds the typist to insert the enclosure in the envelope, and *alerts* the reader that a second document is included in the correspondence. It may indicate the number of enclosures or attachments (Att.), or identify an enclosure specifically (Enclosure: Copy of Invoice 5108).

⟁ Styles of Business Letters

A business letter should be written in a particular style. Basically, there are three common letter styles: Block, Simplified, and Indented.

1. Block Style

The block style is widely used in the business world because of its fast and efficient service, which can actively convey the information of commercial activities. All the lines, including the date line, begin at the left margin. As a result, the writer needn't bother to indent the first line of each sentence, and the time is surely saved. Moreover, the letter looks neat and clean in this style.

Template

_____	LETTERHEAD
_____	DATE
_____	INSIDE ADDRESS
_____	
_____	
_____	SALUTATION
_____	BODY
_____	
_____	
_____	COMPLIMETARY CLOSE
_____	SIGNATURE
_____	ENCLOSURE
_____	

2. Simplified Style

All the lines begin at the left margin, so this style is nearly the same as the block letter with one exception—salutation and complimentary close may disappear in this style, and the writer's name and title are typed in all capitals five lines below the last line of the letter body.

Template

LETTER HEAD

_____	DATE
_____	INSIDE ADDRESS
_____	
_____	SALUTATION
_____	BODY
_____	
_____	
_____	
_____	
_____	
_____	
_____	SIGNATURE

3. Indented Style

The first line of every paragraph starts four spaces from the left-hand margin, and each line of *the inside address* and other parts begins with two or three spaces indented; while the complimentary close and the signature are centered, or on the right-hand side of the sheet.

Template

LETTER HEAD

DATE

INSIDE ADDRESS

SALUTATION

BODY

COMPLIMETARY CLOSE

SIGNATURE

ENCLOSURE

Vocabulary

acquaint	/əˈkweint/	v. 使了解
definition	/ˌdifiˈniʃən/	n. 定义
mark	/mɑːk/	v. 表示；作记号
involve	/inˈvɔlv/	v. 包含；牵涉
classification	/ˌklæsifiˈkeiʃən/	n. 分类；类别
proposal	/prəuˈpəuzəl/	n. 提议，建议
fundamental	/ˌfʌndəˈmentəl/	adj. 基本的，根本的
clarity	/ˈklærəti/	n. 清楚，明晰
correctness	/kəˈrektnis/	n. 正确性
conciseness	/kənˈsaisnis/	n. 简明，简洁
completeness	/kəmˈpliːtnis/	n. 完整，完全
courtesy	/ˈkəːtisi/	n. 礼貌，好意
punctuation	/ˌpʌŋktjuˈeiʃən/	n. 标点符号
conventional	/kənˈvenʃənəl/	adj. 符合习俗的，传统的
concentrate	/ˈkɔnsəntreit/	v. 集中，全神贯注
salutation	/ˌsæljuːˈteiʃən/	n. 称呼；问候

complimentary	/ˌkɔmpli'mentəri/	*adj.* 问候的；称赞的
stationery	/'steiʃənəri/	*n.* 信纸
recipient	/ri'sipiənt/	*n.* 接受者
discourtesy	/dis'kɔːtisi/	*n.* 无礼；粗鲁的言行
enclosure	/in'kləuʒə/	*n.* 附件

 Notes

1. on behalf of... 代表

2. be acquainted with... 对……熟悉

3. take into consideration... 考虑到，顾虑到

4. at the left margin 在页面左边

5. single-space 单行打；double-space 双倍行距，隔行打

6. According to one of the definitions given by *Collins English Dictionary*, writing refers to a group of letters or symbols written or marked on a surface as a means of communicating ideas by making each symbol stand for an idea, concept, or thing.

根据《柯林斯英文词典》给出的定义之一：写作就是使写在或标记在某物表面上的一组字母或符号代表某种观点、概念或某事物，并使其用作交流思想的方式。

7. Therefore, writing is not less important than speaking from the point of view of communicative power.

因此，就其沟通能力而言，写作的重要性并不亚于口头表达。

8. When the receiver interprets the sender's intention and the sender achieves his or her purpose, the writing is considered as an effective one.

当收信人能够读懂写信人的意图，且写信人达到写信目的时，这封信才被视作是一份有效信件。

9. A wordsmith writes in the strongest words, but not necessarily the fewest to achieve the goal.

语言大师常以最有力但不见得是最少的词语来达到简洁的效果。

10. A typical and professional-looking business letter usually includes the following eight elements: the heading, the date, the inside address, the salutation, the letter body, the complimentary close, the signature and the enclosure.

一封典型的专业商务信函通常包括以下八个部分：信头、日期、信内地址、称谓、正文、结尾敬语、签名和附件。

11. The full written form of the month is commonly preferred in case the abbreviation may cause confusion.

一般采用月份的全拼，以免缩写形式引起混淆。

12. In general, the inside address contains the addressee's complete titles and names, which help the recipient route the letter properly if the address on the envelope is unreadable.

一般来说，信内地址包含寄信人的头衔和姓名全称，当信封上的地址不易辨认时，这样有助于收信人按正确地址寄递信函。

13. There are basically three letter styles: Blocked, Simplified, and Indented.

基本上有三种书信格式：齐头式、简化式和缩行式。

Part III
Practical Writing

♦ Practice 1

Work in pairs and answer the following questions.

1. What's the definition of writing?

2. Is speaking more important than writing as far as communication is concerned? Why?

3. What are the three functions of business writing?

4. Does the date position have to be at the left margin between the address and salutation?

5. Is it proper to sign with a rubber stamp rather than to write in ink? Why?

6. What are the three common business letter styles?

♦ Practice 2

Read and Judge (T for True and F for False)

1. Among the four language skills—listening, speaking, reading, and writing, the last one is the least important in respect of its communicative power. (   )

2. Writing plays an important role in both one's life and business. One may write for different purposes, for example, a student may write an essay when his teacher asks him to do so. While a business man may write a notice when he needs to inform his clients of his product performance. (   )

3. You don't need to take care of the punctuation when writing a letter, for it's not as important as the word use. (   )

4. A skillful writer may write in the strongest and fewest words to convey meaning on business occasions because conciseness is one of the key writing principles. (   )

5. It's enough just to include the main data and information in a letter, because other minor information can be omitted. (   )

6. It's unnecessary to type the return address even if it's not been imprinted on the stationery. (   )

7. It's formal and common to write a professional-looking letter only in hand because that represents the sincerity of the writer. (   )

8. According to the letter style, you can either put the complimentary close at the left margin or set its left edge in the center. (   )

9. In most letter styles, the writer's typed name appears three to four lines below the complimentary close, and between them is the hand-written signature. (   )

10. In the indented style, all the lines from the date line begin at the left margin. (   )

Practice 3

Complete the sentences with the proper form of the phrases in the box.

be acquainted with	as a means of	be compared to	from the point of view of
on behalf of	care… about	achieve the goal	take… into consideration

1. An office worker should _____ the computer operation and different kinds of CAD software.

2. It's no easy task to write fiction _____ a living.

3. _____ the quality _____ , I think the price is reasonable.

4. In order to _____ , we will be working whole-heartedly.

5. Our work can _____ a battle, so we must be well prepared for its detail.

6. Mr. Edward is attending the conference _____ the International Trade Association.

7. _____ the country, petrol export is its economic artery.

8. Some customers _____ more _____ the price of the goods than their qualities.

Practice 4

Translate the following sentences.

1. I wish to acknowledge receipt of your order for 30,000 plastic toy portable phones.

2. Employees are generally satisfied with the current benefits package but they requested their classroom payment should be increased.

3. Meet with HMO representatives to discuss the complaints concerning the occupational disease insurance.

4. The letterhead contains the writer's company name, address, telephone and fax number, and e-mail address.

5. The date position depends on the style you choose. It may appear at the left or right margin between the address and salutation.

6. Just as its name implies, "enclosure" means a document that is enclosed to the letter in addition.

Job Vacancies

Objectives

To be proficient in

◎ understanding the useful words and expressions often used in job vacancies

◎ writing job vacancies

◎ using periodic and loose sentences

Cultural Tips

A job vacancy, which is also called employment advertisement, is one of the most effective channels of recruitment. It provides job information through the press, network, television, radio and other mass media in order to attract talented people in line with the requirements of a company.

Just as a résumé creates a first impression to a prospective employer, a job vacancy, as one of the company marketing tools, must be written to attract the ideal candidate for the job.

A job vacancy usually consists of the following parts: company introduction, the position, job description, qualifications, salary and benefits (may be clarified in the interview) and contact information.

Part I
Warm-up Activities

◆ **Work in pairs and write out the main parts involved in a job vacancy.**

What are the main parts?

◆ **Choose the best answer to complete the following job advertisement.**

A. Qualifications & Skills Required

B. Job Description

C. Contact Information

D. Company Introduction

E. Position

Job Offer

1. _____

ASSAB STEELS Malaysia is a subsidiary of a large MNC, listed 590 in Forbes Global 2010. We distribute special tool steel, provide machinery and heat treatment services to our customers. We seek suitably qualified candidates to join us.

2. _____

Indoors Sales Coordinator.

3. _____

To handle work with Tele-sales.

To be able to work closely with outdoors sales team.

4. _____

SPM/STPM or fresh graduates.

Skilled at Word and Excel.

We Have A Job For You

FIRST SOURCE

Recruitment and Consultation

JOBS

HIRING H   RING HI

E-mail : mailbox@firstsource-eg.com

Good communication skills.

1-2 years' work experience is an advantage.

5. _____

Interested applicants can contact Ms. Joanna Tey, fax or apply online with a detailed résumé before 12th Sept., 2011.

The HR Manager

ASSAB STEELS (MALAYSIA)

No 8, Jalan Persiaran Teknologi

Taman Teknologi Johor

81400 Senai, Johor

Tel.: 012-283 5483

Part II
Sample Study

O Sample 1

PERSONAL ASSISTANT

Required for a new company involved in marketing.

Requirements include:

◇ Female, below 35 years

◇ Good *administrative* and secretarial skills

◇ *Minimum* of 2 years relevant experience

Minimum salary RMB 3,000 per month, welfare package to be *negotiated*.

Please reply with a typed résumé to:

Wang Lin

58 Nanjing Road

Shanghai, 210084

O Sample 2

Introduction

PepsiCo (China) Co., Ltd. is an owned foreign enterprise. To cope with our planned expansion in China, we invite talented, *committed* people to join us:

Position

Quality Control Engineer

Qualifications

◇ Male or female aged below 30

◇ Bachelor Degree or above in Quality Control

◇ 2-3 years of relevant work experience in joint venture *preferable*

◇ Good at developing new business relationships

◇ Proficient in using Word & Excel

◇ Preparation for business trips

Interested *candidates* are invited to send your full résumé in both Chinese and English, telephone number and address to:

Personnel Department

PepsiCo (China) Co., Ltd.

Guangzhou Economic & Technical Development District

Guangzhou 510730

Vocabulary

administrative	/əd'ministrətiv/	*adj.* 行政的；管理的
minimum	/'miniməm/	*n.* 最低限度；最小量
negotiate	/ni'gəuʃieit/	*v.* 谈判，磋商，商议
committed	/kə'mitid/	*adj.* 尽心尽力的，忠诚的
preferable	/'prefərəbl/	*adj.* 更好的；更适合的
candidate	/'kændideit/	*n.* 应聘者，应试者

Notes

1. welfare package	福利待遇
2. owned foreign enterprise	独资企业
3. cope with	应付，处理
4. PepsiCo (China) Co., Ltd.	百事可乐（中国）有限公司

Useful Expressions

○ For company introduction

… gain popularity from consumers at home and abroad

... rank first among similar products

... well received by broad users at home and abroad

... touch each and every customer with an exceptional warmth and hospitality

○ For personal qualities

Dynamic, open-minded, capable of being leadership

Excellent interpersonal and presentation skills

Good negotiation skills and a good team player

Young, bright, energetic with a strong career-ambition

○ For diplomas & occupational experience

With about 10 years of relevant work experience

Bachelor degree and above, MBA preferred

○ For proficiency of language and computer skills

Good spoken and written English preferable

Able to speak Mandarin and the Cantonese

Familiar with CAD/CAM preferred

Skilled at Word, Excel, etc.

○ Abbreviations often used in job vacancies

admin: administrative	ad/adv: advertising
agcy: agency	appt: appointment
asst: assistant	clk: clerk
co: company	coll: college
comm: commission	corp: corporation
dept: department	dir: director
evngs: evenings	exp'd: experienced
f/t: full time	hr: hour
hosp: hospital	hdqtrs: headquarters
hrly: hourly	immed: immediate
incl: including	inexp: inexperienced
knowl: knowledge	loc: location
mgr: manager	m-f: Monday-Friday
mth: month	nec: necessary
oppty: opportunity	ot: overtime
perm: permanent	pos: position
eqpt: equipment	p/t: part time
reps: representative	refs: references

req: required

sctry: secretary

typ: typing/typist

wpm: words per minute

sal: salary

temp: temporarily

wk: week/work

yr(s): Year(s)

Part III Practical Writing

Sample Consolidation

♣ Practice 1

Complete the following chart according to the information in samples.

	Sample 1	Sample 2
Headline:	_____	_____
Position:	_____	_____
Qualifications:	_____	_____
Contact information:	_____	_____

Grammar Focus

Periodic Sentences and Loose Sentences

Periodic Sentences

A periodic sentence emphasizes its important point by putting all subordinate clauses and other modifiers before the main sentence. This kind of sentence unfolds gradually so that its main thought becomes available at the end of the sentence. e.g.:

1. Through an extensive network of more than 300,000 agents and over 23,000 employees across 15 geographical markets, the AIA Group （友邦保险集团）serves the holders of over 20 million in-force policies in the region.

2. If you are interested, you can post your résumé written in English and Chinese, and two photos to Miss Mary, secretary of NBA Computer Company.

Loose Sentences

A loose sentence is the sentence in which main thought is given first, followed by clauses or phrases. It may seem informal, loose and conversational. e.g.

1. We are looking for candidates with strong communication skills, who enjoy interacting with people, and can contribute to the company.

2. We have branches in Asia, North America, and Europe, with about 1,000 employees.

❖ Practice 2

Decide which sentences are periodic sentences (PS) and wihich ones are loose sentences (LS).

(   ) 1. Being well acquainted with office work, I could make myself generally useful.

(   ) 2. There are several posts available and long-term prospects are good, though initially all successful applicants will be contracted for a maximum of 9 months.

(   ) 3. We are looking for an individual with relevant academic training and experience who could serve as office assistant in our Changsha branch.

(   ) 4. If you'd like to work in an organization with a vibrant culture and working environment, we'd like to hear from you.

(   ) 5. If I am elected as President, I will not let you down.

(   ) 6. We need a full package of your documents when you apply for the job.

(   ) 7. The AIA Group is a leading life insurance organization in Asia Pacific that traces its roots in the region back more than 90 years.

(   ) 8. We help begin lasting relationships with their new customers by taking time to meet with them in person where they work, live and shop.

❖ Practice 3

Change the following loose sentences into periodic sentences.

1. Shenzhen Research Institute, Sun Yat-sen University is located in an ultra modern metropolitan area with a population of 15 million near the border of Hong Kong.

2. Miss Tracy Lee will graduate from Shanghai Institute of Tourism this fall, finishing her three-year study of tourism management.

3. I offer proficiency in telecom software development in addition to my knowledge of business processes.

4. He decided to apply for the position of English teacher though he was interested in music.

5. My roommate asked me to fill in a job vacancy for him when I came off the work.

6. I will take up the accountant position though I am not interested in it.

Language Points

❖ Practice 4

Match each word with the correct definition.

1. enterprise   a. relating to the work of managing a company or organization

2. candidate   b. likely to develop into a particular type of person or thing in the future

3. administrative   c. a person who has the authority to carry out administrative or managerial duties

4. executive   d. a business venture or company

5. potential   e. a person who is seen as suitable for a position

6. preferable   f. more desirable than another

1. _____ 2. _____ 3. _____ 4. _____ 5. _____ 6. _____

♣ Practice 5

Complete the following sentences with the proper form of the words or phrases in the box.

executive	resource	qualify	negotiate	package

1. You'll never get a good job if you don't have any _____.

2. We offer a competitive welfare _____ which will commensurate with qualifications and experience.

3. She is now a senior _____, having worked her way up through the company.

4. Everything is _____ at this stage—I'm ruling nothing out.

5. She's a very _____ manager.

♣ Practice 6

Complete the following sentences in English.

1. Experience with agricultural equipment _____(优先).

2. The company had _____(年销售量) of US$ 160 million and our business is growing up rapidly.

3. The job holder will have _____(三年以上的行政工作经验).

4. _____(团队合作) was the key to their success.

5. _____(熟练使用Word) is the basic skill you should have.

Letter Practice

TEMPLATE

> **Headline:** _____ of the job vacancy
>
> **Company Description:** _____ of the company with a brief description of the nature of the business
>
> **Job Title:** the _____ needed
>
> **Job DescRription:** main _____
>
> **Job Requirements/Qualifications:** _____ and experience, etc.
>
> **Contact Information:** e-mail or telephone number, etc.

♣ Practice 7

Compose a job vacancy with the given information according to the template above.

A. improve the day-to-day operational efficiency of the business

B. taking charge of housekeeping issues and help-desk operations

C. The company is looking for a polished individual

D. acting as a point of contact and support for visitors and associates

E. A leading investment management group

Office Support Services

(1) _____ is looking to hire an individual to provide office support services to associate within their London office. The role is a challenging and varied one, and focuses on ensuring that the services provided are maintained to a high standard, as well as (2) _____.

Responsibilities for this role include coordinating routine maintenance and services, providing and ensuring daily operational service or assistance, (3) _____, and recommending and initiating new procedures to improve efficiency, quality and timeliness of services. In addition to this, the role also involves some project work, where you can become involved in analyzing data and trends to identify potential problems, as well as working with managers and senior managers to set priorities and support initiatives, and (4) _____.

(5) _____ who is personable, enthusiastic and possesses a strong customer focus, with the clear ability to establish and maintain effective working relationships across all levels.

♣ Practice 8

Complete the following advertisement according to the Chinese in the parentheses.

The Air Liquid Company of France (1) _____ （是西欧最大的石油、天然气开发、销售商）. Besides providing fuel oil for European countries, it has taken pains to build a series of laboratories for hi-tech petrol-chemical research and development. (2) _____ （现诚聘一名化验师）.

Qualifications:

Active involvement in our ISO 9001 certified quality system.

(3) _____ （能从事产品的研发）.

(4) _____ （良好的团队精神）.

(5) _____ （理想的应聘者还需具备两年的相关经验）and hold a valid Chemistry qualification.

Send application, résumé and letter of recommendation to:

14 Avenue Berthelot

69361 Lyon Cedex 07

France

◆ Practice 9

Write a job vacancy according to the following situation, adding details where necessary.

Brilliant Hotel是杭州一家五星级酒店，现需招聘一名酒店经理，招聘条件如下：

女性，年龄不超过35岁；大学本科以上学历，主修酒店管理或相关专业；至少有3年以上酒店管理经验；有良好的交际能力；熟练使用Word和Excel；英语和普通话流利者优先。

请有意者在一个月内将中英文简历及大学毕业证书的电子件发至dan@sanderson.com。

Part IV
Supplementary Reading

Reading One

Administrative Assistant—Part-time

About McDonald's

McDonald's is the largest and best-known global food-serve retailer with more that 30,000 restaurants, serving 46 million customers each day in 118 countries. We plan to expand our leadership position through tasty food, superior service, everyday value and convenience. Join our team and find out firsthand why *Fortune* magazine calls us one of America's most admired companies.

Position

This is a part-time job-sharing position (20 hours per week with benefits). Work time is Wednesday afternoon, Thursday and Friday.

Responsibilities

◇ Opening, sorting and distributing incoming mails, reports and correspondences

◇ Arranging travel reservations and accommodation

◇ Processing telephone calls and answering enquires

Key Requirements

◇ High school diploma or above required

◇ Minimum of 3 years' administrative experience

◇ Strong project management and organizational skills

◇ Teamwork skills

◇ Excellent written and verbal skills in English

◇ Proficient in Word, Excel and PowerPoint

Reading Two

LSG Sky Chefs （汉莎天厨）is one of the large airline catering company world-wide by serving about 260 airlines from our 200 different locations in over 40 countries on all continents with everything that makes flying pleasant. This success is achieved by our professional logistics infrastructure, newest techniques and highly qualified personnel.

To cope with the rapid expansion in China, we now invite applications for the following position to be stationed in China.

Position

Station Managers (China)

Duties

The incumbent is accountable for overseeing, directing and controlling all operative activities at one of our Flight Kitchen in China. He/she has to plan and carry out the duties and responsibilities with a view to maximizing on-time performance and efficiency and ensuring the satisfaction of airline Clients.

Requirements

◇ Bachelor Degree or above in Hotel & Catering Management (餐饮管理);

◇ At least 3 years' experience in supervisory level or 6 years' relevant experience in catering industry, and overseas work experience is preferable;

◇ Excellent communication skills;

◇ Good command in both written and spoken English and Chinese (Mandarin).

We offer an attractive remuneration package (福利条件) in commensurate with the qualifications to the ideal candidate. Interested parties please apply with full résumé to recruit@lsgskychefs.com.cn.

Lesson Three •●●

Résumé

Objectives

To be proficient in
◎ the useful words and expressions often used in a *résumé*
◎ writing a résumé
◎ using parallel structure

Cultural Tips

A résumé (also curriculum vitae/CV) is a brief introduction of yourself with a list of your personal information written in a particular format, whose purpose is to help you land an interview for a job. Therefore, a good résumé means employment is likely to be more successful, characterized by conciseness and completeness, usually covering no more than two pages. The following information is generally included in a résumé: your personal data (name, address and contact way); job *objective*; education; work experience; skills/awards; references.

Part I
Warm-up Activities

◆ **Work in pairs and find out the best answer to the reasons for writing a résumé.**

For practicing writing skills

Just for fun

For getting an opportunity of job interview

◆ **Read the following résumé and fill in the blanks with the missing information marked from A to D.**

    A. References

    B. Education

    C. Work Experience

    D. Employment Objective

Su Jiayuan

16 Harong Rd., Changsha, 410000

(0731) 3673358

sjy@yahoo.com

_____

To work as an accountant, leading to a management position

_____

Bachelor's Degree in Accounting from Hunan University of Finance and Economics, June 2004

Certificates: Certified Public Accountant (CPA) and Certified Management Accountant (CMA)

_____

2009—present

Financial accounting assistant in Ouyi Flourmill Factory, Changsha

Review and correct accounting entries.

Prepare company accounts and tax returns for audit.

2005—2009

Accountancy Clerk in Quandemiao Bread Slices Company

Recorded and monitored company expenses.

Computer Skills

Skilled at using Excel, Access, Word, PowerPoint

_____

Zhang Yun Head Accountant, Quandemiao Bread Slices Company, (0731) 8223799

Li Lanxin Sales Manager, Ouyi Flourmill Factory, Changsha, (0731) 8417235

Part II
Sample Study

Sample 1

Feng Lu

Contact

19 Liming Eastern Street, Linhe Dist., Bayannuer, Inner Mongolia, 015000

(0478) 8417266

Job Objective

English teacher in primary or middle schools

Education

Bachelor Degree in English Literature, Hetao University (June 2012)

Certificates and Awards

CET-6 (2011)

The first prize in the English Speech Contest held by Foreign Language Department of Hetao University (2011)

First-class *Scholarship*, Foreign Language Department of Hetao University (2010)

Experience in Teaching English

Teach students of Grade Five English in NO. 6 Primary School of Linhe. (2011.09—2012.01)

Teach middle school students English in Cambridge English Training Center of Linhe (2011.06—2011.08)

Skills

Fluent in English

Excellent in Word, Excel, and PowerPoint

10 secrets to a successful job search

Sample 2

Wen Jianying

16 Furong Rd. Changsha, Hunan, 410000

0731- 36558833

Employment Objective

To obtain a position as an *accountant* in a large corporation

Work Experience

2008—present Financial Accounting Assistant in Hetao Wine Co., Ltd.

Preparing routine entries and post financial *transactions*

Creating budgets and forecasts for the management group

Preparing company accounts and tax returns for *audit*

2004—2008 Accounting Clerk in Fangfang Cake Factory

Administered online banking functions

Managed payroll function for 80 employees

Recorded and monitored company expenses

Qualifications

Have general knowledge of accountancy, as well as the experience of accountant transaction

Own strong management experience with extensive knowledge in statistical processes

Possess excellent computer and communication skills

Education Experience

Bachelor's Degree in Accounting from the Finance and Economics Institute of Jiangxi, June 2003

Certificate

Certified Public Accountant (CPA)

Special Skills

Good skills in Word, Excel and PowerPoint

References

Available on request

Vocabulary

résumé	/'rezjuːmei/	n. 履历，个人简历
objective	/əb'dʒektiv/	n. 目标，目的
scholarship	/'skɔləʃip/	n. 奖学金
accountant	/ə'kauntənt/	n. 会计师，会计人员
transaction	/træn'zækʃən/	n. 交易，事务
audit	/'ɔːdit/	n. 审计
administer	/əd'ministə/	v. 管理，执行
certificate	/sə'tifikeit/	n. 证书

Notes

1. Certified Public Accountant (CPA) 注册会计师
2. Bachelor Degree in English Literature 英语文学学士学位
3. English Speech Contest 英语演讲比赛

4. Cambridge English Training Center 剑桥英语培训中心
5. post financial transactions 公布账务收支情况

 Expressions

○ For describing job objectives

To seek/obtain/get/secure a position as...

An entry-level position responsible for...

Position desired/applied for...

A position requiring...

○ For presenting education

graduated from... majoring in...

additional training and qualifications

academic preparation for...

useful courses for... include...

○ For introducing work experience

I have gained a good knowledge of...

I have acquired a broad concept of the business world from...

worked/served as... in...

accountable/responsible for...

in charge of...

○ For showing qualifications

possessed/attained the skills that...

got the higher qualifications that ...

recognized for...

awarded by...

○ For providing skills

A good command of... skill

Strong analytical and problem solving skills

Excellent skills in...

○ For offering references

Available upon request

References and a portfolio/transcript of... will be furnished on request

Part III
Practical Writing

Sample Consolidation

♣ Practice 1

Complete the following information according to the samples.

	Sample 1	Sample 2
Name:	_____	_____
Address:	_____	_____
Job Objectives:	_____	_____
Education:	_____	_____
Work Experience:	_____	_____
Skills:	_____	_____

Grammar Focus
Parallelism

Parallelism (parallel structure), derived from ancient Greek, is a rhetorical device commonly used to give clarity, rhythm and force to a sentence with two or more similar grammatical structures, meaning side by side and balancing each other. For instance, a noun is listed with other nouns, an adjective with other adjectives, and so on. Failure to express such items in identical grammatical form is regarded as faulty parallelism. There are four types of parallel structure: word parallel, phrase parallel, clause parallel, sentence parallel. e.g.:

His girl partner is beautiful, enthusiastic and intelligent. (word parallel)

To say with lips is easy, but to do with hands is difficult. (phrase parallel)

What you say and what I see are inconsistent. (clause parallel)

The love of liberty is the love of others; the love of power is the love of ourselves. (sentence parallel)

♣ Practice 2

Choose the best answer to complete the parallel structure below.

1. To answer the phones and _____ the visitors are my routines.

    A. meet   B. to meet   C. meeting   D. met

2. Speech is silver, but _____ is gold.

    A. silence   B. no to speak   C. silent   D. being silent

3. My education, _____ and my ability make me confident of the position.

    A. the work experience   B. I have lots of experience in my work

    C. experienced   D. my work experience

4. He has immense interpersonal skills, proficient spoken English and _____, so he will become a good English teacher.

   A. patient   B. patience

   C. enough patient   D. enough patience

5. I came; I saw; _____.

   A. to conquer   B. I conquer

   C. I conquered   D. conquered

6. I hate him not for his cruelty, _____.

   A. for his greed   B. but for he is greedy

   C. because of his greed   D. but for his greed

7. A man _____ and who is responsible for his family is respected and loved.

   A. who does his work actively   B. that actively does his work well

   C. who is active in his work   D. that is good at his work

8. The heroine in *The Tale of White Snake* _____.

   A. wants freedom and to find love   B. longs for freedom and love

   C. want free life and love   D. longs for being free and true love

9. Yesterday the fans in the auditorium _____ for more shows.

   A. to clap and to scream   B. clapping and screaming

   C. clapped and screamed   D. clap and scream

10. I love you as much as the Grey Wolf _____.

   A. love himself   B. loves his wife

   C. loved his wife   D. to love himself

♣ Practice 3

Change the following sentences into sentences with parallel structure.

1. He applies for the job not only because of its high salary, but it has bright future.

2. We can't help but believe that the old hatreds shall someday pass. The lines of tribe will soon dissolve.

3. There was no smile on his lips, and there wasn't any generosity in his eyes either.

4. This great nation will endure as it has endured, will revive and it's going to prosper.

5. Comparatively, the price of the soft drink is much cheaper than that of Cola, and it has a better taste.

Language Points

♣ Practice 4

Match each word to the correct definition.

1. résumé   a. a high degree of ability or skill in something

2. major   b. an ability or quality that you need in order to do a particular job

3. proficiency   c. a summary of your academic and work history

4. interpersonal   d. someone whose job is to help another person in their work

5. qualification   e. involving relationships between people

6. assistant   f. an official document or record stating that particular facts are true

7. certificate   g. a student's main subject at college or university

8. objective   h. the goal intended to be attained

1. _____   2. _____   3. _____   4. _____

5. _____   6. _____   7. _____   8. _____

❖ Practice 5

Complete the following sentences with the proper form of the words in the box.

interpersonal	major	energy	administer	award	analyze	available	contribute

1. A successful leader should have strong _____ skills.

2. We formed the organization specifically to _____ the project.

3. The city could not have been prosperous without the valuable _____ from the migrant workers.

4. The sales staff should learn how to _____ the market and develop marketing planning.

5. Tess is a girl with much _____. In this regard, she is competent to do the job.

6. I'm _____ this Wednesday if you want to meet me then.

7. —What was your _____ at the university?

    —Political Science.

8. Students will be _____ a diploma if they can complete all the courses successfully.

❖ Practice 6

Complete the following sentences in English.

1. I _____(已获得管理经验) and communication skills through part-time employments.

2. The purpose of a résumé is to _____(使你获得面试机会).

3. I am _____(寻求会计部门的一个职位) where I can use my financial training to solve business problems.

4. _____ (你简历的格式和内容) depend on your qualifications, the job field and personality you wish to describe.

5. A résumé is mainly a data sheet with _____(列有学历、工作经历) and skills, etc.

Language Points

TEMPLATE

Contact Information: the _____ on how you are reached

Objective: the _____ (or type of work) you are seeking

Qualifications: the knowledge, skills, certificates or awards specifically essential to the position

Education: _____ and _____ you've graduated, what degrees you've got, what courses you've taken, etc.

Work Experience: information on _____ you've done, and when and where you've worked.

References: your references' information to show you are well prepared for the job

♣ Practice 7

Complete the résumé with the following parts according to the template above.

A. Keeping the office running effectively; duties include typing, making and answering calls, dealing with the visitors, arranging appointment, etc.

B. Receptionist, in Datong government office

C. Studied in Datong Secretarial School, Datong, China
   Majored in Secretarial Science Courses contained: Typing, Filing, Shorthand, and Office Software Operation

D. To get a position as an executive secretary in a foreign company

---

Li Wencheng

22 Jianshe Street Baotou, Inner Mongolia, 014000

(0472)86960832

Objective

(1) _____

Education

Sept. 2000-July 2003

(2) _____

Work Experience

June 2007 to Present

Secretary, the Branch of Haier Company in Datong

(3) _____

Sept. 2003 to May 2007

(4) _____

Special Skills

Typing—30 w.p.m.

Shorthand—130 w.p.m.

Fluent in Chinese, English, Mongolian

Proficient in Word 2007, Excel, Powerpoint

References

Ms. Fang Meiling, Office Manager, the Branch of Haier Company in Datong, 18 Nanhai Road Caiyuan District, Datong, 037000, (0352) 86368822

Mr. Sun Xuejun, Personnel Director, Datong Government Office, 362 East Street, Datong 037000, (0352) 85623997.

✤ Practice 8

Complete the résumé below according to the Chinese in the parentheses.

Zhao Linlin

Address until July, 2011   Permanent Address（永久地址）

P.O. BOX 169# Hetao University   580 Caobao Road

Inner Mongolia   Nanjing, 210000

0471(015000)   (025) 83358328

Objective: (1)_____(教中学生英语)

Education:

(2)_____(英语教育学士学位) from Hetao University, June 2011

Courses contained: Intensive Reading, Listening, English Literature, Oral English, Teaching Methodology, Translatology

Teaching Experience:

(3)_____（兼职英语家教）(in summer holiday of 2010)

English teacher in New Cambridge English Club in Linhe City (from Jan. 2011 to the present)

Certificates: CET-6; Teaching Certificate

Skills: (4)_____(英语口语流利)；Skilled at communication

Personality: Confident, patient, outstanding

References: (5) _____(如有要求，随时提供)

✤ Practice 9

Read the following résumé, and write a brief one for yourself according to your real situation.

Résumé

Name: He Minxia

Address: Room 202, Building 2, Caiyuan Housing District, Huhhot, Inner Mongolia, 010010

E-mail: hmx@sohu.com

Telephone: 0471-7902268

Work Experience:

July 1999—the present

    Secretary to the Manager at Shandong Branch, Hongle Toy Co., Ltd.

Sept. 1996—June 1999

    Office Clerk at Finance and Trade Vocational School

Education Background:

Sept. 1992—July 1996

    Majored in Business at Inner Mongolia Finance and Economics Institute

Sept. 1990—July 1992

    Studied at No.1 High School of Bayannuer, Inner Mongolia

Awards:

2010 Outstanding Contribution to Hongle Toy Co., Ltd.

1995 "Excellent Student Leader" of Inner Mongolia Finance and Economics Institute

Certificates: CET- 4; BEC (Intermediate)

Part IV
Supplementary Reading

Reading One

What Is a Résumé?

A résumé is a brief introduction of yourself. Its purpose is to help you land a job interview. The word "résumé" is derived from French, meaning "to summarize". In some dictionaries, it

is defined as "a summary of one's work experience and educational background". Generally, a résumé is written for getting a new employment. At that point, a successful résumé needs your time and brain cells to accomplish. So, before you start writing, it makes sense to sort over your thoughts and to make it clear where your strengths and weaknesses are so that you can enhance your strong points and avoid the weaknesses.

A typical résumé includes the following elements:

Personal data—including your name, address, phone number (fax number as well if any), e-mail address. The more detailed, the better.

Job objective—provide the position or the type of work you are applying for.

Work experience—offer the information of what your job was, where and when you worked.

Education—inform the reader of where and when you graduated, what degree you've got, and of what courses you've taken.

Skills—list skills that are helpful to get the desired job.

References—provide the information of your references to indicate what you've offered is from the proper source.

Reading Two

Chronological Résumé and Functional Résumé

The main types of résumés include chronological résumé and functional résumé. The former is in the traditional organization format, which is arranged in chronological order, beginning with the most recent, so it is called the chronological résumé. While the latter is a functional résumé, which focuses on the function and the nature of the work instead of the chronological order. Read the following two samples, and note the differences between them.

Chronological Résumé

Zhao Yanli

18 Lushan St., Shenzhen, China, 501788

(0755) 28368899, zyl@sohu.com

Job Objective

To obtain a position as a Human Resources Manager

Education

2003.09—2007.07 Peking University

2000.09—2003.07 High School affiliated to Peking University

Major Courses

Business Information System, Business Law, Industrial Psychology, Marketing, International Business, Business Strategy, etc.

Related Experience

2007.10—the present Administrative Assistant to the Vice-President, Shenzhen Insurance Company

Certificates

CET-6

Bachelor in Business Administration

Associate Degree in Human Resources Management Division

Awards

Got scholarship for "Top Student" in Peking University (twice)

References

Available upon request

Functional Résumé

Danniel Smith

Campus Address: Permanent Address:

328 West Hill Road   803 Oak Street

Missouri University 36676   Monroe City, Missouri 365677

(680) 2986009   (681) 2091236

Career Objective

An English teacher, to convey an enthusiasm for English learning to students

Qualifications

Immense skills for teaching English; EXCELLENT TEACHER Prize for two years from IELTS Training House, Missouri

Service-oriented Education

Bachelor in British Literature of Missouri University (September 2006 to March 2009)

Additional Coursework in education: Educational Psychology, French, Computer Science, and Methodology

Achievements

Received English Department Award for Outstanding Scholarship (2008)

Personal Information

Have a good command of both spoken and written English

Additional Information

Letters of references are available upon request

Lesson Four •••

Cover Letters

Objectives

To be proficient in
◎ the useful words and expressions often used in cover letters
◎ writing cover letters
◎ maintaining consistency between the subject and the verb

Cultural Tips

A cover letter is sometimes called an application letter. As a kind of business letter, it's essential in job-hunting. Its content is dependent upon the applicant's desired position and individual information. Generally, it should include these main points: how you got to know this vacancy and the purpose of the letter; personal information; reasons for applying for this position; your wish to obtain an opportunity of interview at the end of the letter.

Part I
Warm-up Activities

◆ **Imagine you will graduate from college next year, and you want to find a job in the field of import and export trade. What are you going to prepare among the following items?**

> *Invitation Letter*
> *Résumé*
> *Congratulation Letter*
> *Cover Letter*

◆ **Choose the appropriate answers and put them in correct order.**

What are the essential parts in a cover letter?

A. Personal information

B. Demand for high salary

C. Your wish to obtain an opportunity of interview

D. Reasons for applying for the position

E. Complaining about or criticizing your former boss

F. How you got to know the vacancy

G. Purpose of writing the letter

Part II
Sample Study

Sample 1

March 15, 2011

Personnel Department
Guangzhou Light Industrial Products Imp. & Exp. Co., Ltd
9F, No. 67, Changdi Road, Yuexiu
Guangzhou, 510120

Dear Sir/Madam,

I'm writing to express my *desire* to apply for your recently advertised position for Assistant Manager.

I graduated from Tianjin Science & Technology University in 2009, where I gained a good foundation of Business English. I have been working for 2 years as an office clerk at a joint venture. I have extensive experience in many related fields. The reason for leaving my present employment is that I desire to improve myself.

The enclosed résumé will tell you more about me. Should you *entertain* my application favorably, I will spare no trouble to acquit myself to your satisfaction.

I would welcome the opportunity for a personal interview with you at your convenience.

Sincerely yours,

Lili Wang
Lili Wang
Enclosures

Sample 2

School of Business
Hunan University of Science & Technology
Taoyuan Road, Xiangtan, Hunan

April 10, 2011
Human Resources Manager
Shanghai Shida Trading Co., Ltd
No. 64 Mid Longhai Road, Shanghai

Dear Sir or Madam,

From the website of your company, I found out your need for an *agent* in Changsha. I am very interested in this position, and I believe I can meet your requirements.

I will get my master's degree in Marketing in Hunan University of Science & Technology in June. While working toward my master's degree, I served as a sales representative in Amway Corporation where my sales volume was highly praised. I would like to repeat that success in your company.

Enclosed is a copy of my *curriculum vitae*, which fully details my qualifications for the position.

I would appreciate the *privilege* of an interview. I may be reached by telephone at 0731-58290011.

Thank you for your time and attention.

Yours sincerely,

Mary Li

Mary Li

Encl.

Vocabulary

desire	/di'zaiə/	*n.* 心愿，要求
entertain	/ˌentə'tein/	*v.* 考虑
agent	/'eːdʒənt/	*n.* 代理人，代理商
privilege	/'privilidʒ/	*n.* 特权；优惠

Notes

1. Light Industrial Products Imp. & Exp. Co., Ltd.	轻工业品进出口有限公司
2. joint venture	合资企业
3. spare no trouble	不遗余力
4. Amway Corporation	安利公司
5. sales volume	销售量
6. curriculum vitae=résumé	〈拉〉简历表，履历

Useful Expressions

❍ For applying for the position

I'm writing to apply for your recently advertised position for...

With reference/In reply to your advertisement in... I offer myself for the position.

○ For expecting an interview

I hope that you will be kind enough to consider my application favorably.

I would welcome the opportunity for a personal interview with you at your convenience.

Should you entertain my application favorably, I would spare no trouble to acquit myself to your satisfaction.

Should you give me a trial, I will do my utmost to afford you every satisfaction.

Part III Practical Writing

Sample Consolidation

♣ Practice 1

Complete the following chart according to the information in the samples.

	Sample 1	Sample 2
Applicant:	_____	_____
Recipient:	_____	_____
Job objective:	_____	_____
Source of the news:	_____	_____
Education:	_____	_____
Experience:	_____	_____

Grammar Focus

Consistency Between the Subject and the Verb

In English, it's important that the subject should be consistent with the verb, i.e., if the subject is singular, so is the verb; and if the subject is plural, the verb should also be plural. Subject –verb consistency principles can be summarized from the following aspects.

1. Taking a singular verb

(1) If the *v-ing form, indefinite or clause* is used as a subject, the verb is singular.

e.g.: What you should urgently do at present is to do your utmost to dispatch the goods without any delay.

(2) If indefinite pronouns such as *anyone, anybody, anything, everyone, everybody, everything, someone, somebody, something, no one, nobody, nothing* and *each* are used as subjects, the verbs should be in singular form.

e.g.: Everyone, men or women, old or young, enjoys sports and games.

(3) If a subject refers to *time, money, distance, price, measurement*, etc., which is regarded as a whole, the verb is singular.

e.g.: The 199 tons of peanuts *has* been consigned to you per s.s " Dongfeng".

(4) If the subject nouns connected by *and* are modified by *each* or *every*, the verb is in singular form.

e.g.: Each boy and each girl *wants* to go to visit the exhibition.

(5) If the two subject nouns connected by *and* refer to the same thing, the verb should be singular.

e.g.: The secretary and driver is very busy now.

2. Taking a plural verb

(1) If the two subject nouns connected by *and* refer to different things, the verb should be plural.

e.g.: The enclosed illustrated catalogue and samples *were* sent to you a day ago.

(2) If the subject is a collective noun, such as *people, police, cattle*, etc., the verb should be plural.

e.g.: Cattle sell well in the country market at present according to the evening news.

(3) If the subject is formed by a *number of, quantities* of + *plural noun*, the verb is in plural form.

e.g.: Large quantities of beer *are* consumed in the city every year.

3. Taking either a plural verb or a singular verb

If a subject is a collective noun, the verb may be either singular or plural. If it focuses on the whole, the verb is in singular form; if it focuses on the members, the verb is in plural form.

e.g.: The family *are* fond of music.

The family *is* a happy one.

4. Other principles

(1) If the subjects are nouns connected by *either…or, neither…nor, not only…but also, whether…or*, the verb is decided by the noun which is the closest to it.

e.g.: Neither the company president nor the sales managers *are* college graduates.

Either you or I am to take up the work.

(2) If a subject is followed by *with, along with, together with, as well as, besides, except, but, without*, etc., the verb is decided by the real subject before these phrases.

e.g.: Professor Smith, along with his assistants, is working on the project day and night to meet the deadline.

E-mail, as well as telephone, is playing an important part in daily communications.

❖ Practice 2

Complete the sentences with the proper form of the words in the parentheses.

1. Letters of credit _____ (be) the most common form of international payment because they provide a high degree of protection for both the buyer and the seller.

2. Your name and address _____ (have) been given to us by Messrs. J. Smith & Co., Inc. in New York.

3. The high reputation you enjoy _____ (have) rendered us desirous of entering into business relationships with you.

4. What we can do best _____ (be) to meet you halfway.

5. If any of the items in the catalogue _____ (meet) your interest, please let us have your specific enquiry.

6. We hope these terms _____ (be) satisfactory and look forward to your order.

7. All her funds _____ (be) tied up in investing in the real estate.

8. We regret that there _____ (be) several points in the L/C not in conformity with what are stipulated in the contract as follows.

◆ Practice 3

Correct the errors in the following sentences.

1. A number of applicants is waiting for being interviewed by the personnel manager now.

2. Packing list showing gross and net weights are required.

3. A new consignment of goods have just arrived.

4. Direct steamers from here to your port is few and far between.

5. My knowledge of computers and business go beyond my formal classroom education.

6. The Chamber of Commerce of China have conveyed to us your desire to establish business relations with foreign trade corporations.

7. Loss are due to careless packing.

8. You can rest assured that the quality of the goods turn out to your satisfaction.

9. Retailing price for your bicycles here have also been reduced by 5%.

10. Everything appear to be correct and in good condition except in Case No. 40.

Language Points

◆ Practice 4

Match each word to the correct definition.

1. résumé   a. consider, calculate

2. entertain   b. to want something very much

3. desire   c. a formal meeting at which someone is asked questions in order to find out whether they are suitable for a job

4. privilege   d. a right or advantage that you have and others may not have

5. interview   e. a short written account of your education and your previous jobs that you send to an employer when you are looking for a new job

1._____ 2._____ 3._____ 4._____ 5._____

♣ Practice 5

Complete the following sentences with the proper form of the words in the box.

privilege	reputation	consider	interview	desire	contribution

1. Your participation will _____ a lot to our future cooperation.

2. I would appreciate the _____ of an interview.

3. We have built a solid _____ for providing quality workmanship and superior service at a fair price.

4. My reason for leaving my present employment is that I am _____ of getting broader experience in trading.

5. I can discuss in _____ detail my close relationships with key executives at companies such as Guangda, Honghe.

6. I am looking forward to meeting you in person and will call next for an _____.

♣ Practice 6

Complete the following sentences in English.

1. _____ (我写信应聘) the post of salesman as advertised in *China Daily* of May 21.

2. _____ (正如您从简历中看到的), I have participated in various activities and acquired experiences which have helped prepare me for the customer service representative position.

3. Should you give me a trial, I will do my utmost to _____ (以满足贵公司的要求).

4. If given the opportunity, I would _____ (成为公司的得力干将).

5. _____ (附函附寄的个人简历可让您了解我更多的个人情况), which, I believe, will qualify me to become a member of your sales force.

Letter Practice

TEMPLATE

Date:

Employer's Contact Information:

Salutation:

Body:

Tell that you are applying for the job and the information _____.

Explain your _____ for the job (such as your education, skills and experience).

Give thanks and the _____ of being interviewed.

♣ Practice 7

Compose a cover letter with the given information according to the template above.

A. Thank you for your time and consideration

B. I am teaching is limited to the basics

C. it should be an ideal place to improve myself

D. I am grateful for taking some of your time with this unexpected letter

E. give me a reply at your earliest convenience

December 26, 2011

Personnel Office

Pacific Computer Company

Tianjin, 200039

Dear Sir or Madam,

(1) _____ . I am writing to inquire if there are vacancies in your company for computer experts. I graduated from Zhejiang University in 2010, majoring in Computer Science. After graduation I have been working at Beijing Technical School. As the scope of the courses (2) _____ , I wish to have a new job in which I can use the advanced knowledge of computers I acquired at my university and familiarize myself with the new developments in this field.

Since your company is well known for the computers it produces, (3) _____ . I hope you will kindly consider my application and (4) _____ .

Enclosed please find my résumé and three references written by my former professors and the principal of the technical school where I am working.

(5) _____ .

Yours respectfully,

Li Lan

Enclosure

♣ Practice 8

Complete the following letter according to the Chinese in the parentheses.

March 20, 2011

Dear Sir or Madam,

(1) _____ (对广告招聘销售经理一职很感兴趣) in yesterday's *Daily Telegraph* and (2) _____ (希望您能考虑让我担任这一职位) .

My full particulars are shown in my enclosed résumé, from which you will know that I

(3) _____ (有10年的销售经验) in a well-known company. I thoroughly enjoy my work in Phoenix Plastics Ltd., but think that (4) _____ (该换工作发展自己的时候了) because my experience in marketing has prepared me for the responsibility of full sales management.

(5) _____ (如需要，我乐意提供任何其他信息) and I look forward to hearing from you.

Yours faithfully,
Chen Dan
Chen Dan

♣ Practice 9

Write a cover letter according to the following information, adding details where necessary.

Your name is Li Can. You will graduate from Department of Physics, Beijing University of Posts & Telecommunications in June, 2013. During college study you showed great interest in electric circuits and vacuum tubes. Now you are writing to TCL Communications Apparatus Company Ltd. to apply for a position of communication engineer. You will submit the cover letter to the following address:

South Eling Road, Huizhou, Guangdong, 516001
TCL Communication Apparatus Company Ltd.

Part Ⅳ
Supplementary Reading

Reading One

March 28, 2011

Dear Sir/Madam,

In response to your advertisement on your website, I wish to apply as an engineer for network maintenance in your company. I have confidence in meeting the requirements of your company.

In July this year, I will be graduating from Xiamen University with a master degree in Computer Science. My college study has equipped me with a profound professional knowledge of computers. Not only have I passed CET-4, but more importantly, I can speak English fluently. In addition, I have access to scholarships. I also served as Chairman of the Students' Union, and have a strong ability

to organize and coordinate. A strong sense of enterprise and responsibility makes me capable of facing difficulties and challenges. Should you entertain my application favorably, I would like contribute to the development of your company.

The enclosed résumé will tell you more about my personal information, including my references, to whom I can refer you as to my character and ability. I shall be glad to be called at any time for an interview.

Yours faithfully,

Xie Kailong

Xie Kailong

Reading Two

Dear Mr. Nelson,

Susan, your Personnel Officer, has told me that you have a vacancy for a marketing assistant. I would like to be considered for this post.

As you will see from my enclosed résumé, I have been a shorthand typist in the Marketing Department of Sunlight Cables Ltd. for two years. I have been very happy there and have gained a lot of valuable experience. However, the company is quite small and I now wish to broaden my experience and hopefully improve my prospects.

My present employer has written the enclosed reference and has kindly agreed to give further details if you are interested in my application.

I am able to attend an interview at any time and hope to hear from you soon.

Yours sincerely,

Jean Carson

Jean Carson

Encls: Résumé
        Reference letter

Unit 2

Social Correspondence

商务交际

Invitation Letters

Objectives

To be proficient in
- ◎ understanding the useful words and expressions often used in invitation letters
- ◎ writing invitation letters
- ◎ using It-cleft sentences

Cultural Tips

A business invitation letter is relatively formal. The tone should be polite and enthusiastic. It usually includes the following content: showing the intention of asking the invitee to attend and the related information of the activities such as name, time, place, event, etc.; then expressing the sincerity of hoping the other party will attend and expecting the recipient to give a reply.

Part I
Warm-up Activities

◆ **Work in pairs and write out the key elements included in an invitation letter.**

◇ Intention of invitation
◇ _____
◇ Hope of a reply

◆ **Write out the relevant information with reference to the invitation letter below.**

Dear Mr. & Mrs. S. Lewis,

We request the honor of your presence at the opening ceremony of our company on Sunday, the first of May at eleven o'clock in Shanghai International Hotel.

Yours sincerely,
Thomas

Inviter: _____   Invitee: _____   Activity: _____

Part II
Sample Study

◯ Sample 1

Dear Sir or Madam,

China National Sugar and Alcoholic Commodities Fair, *sponsored* by the China National Sugar and Alcohol Group Corp., is held twice yearly in spring and autumn *respectively*, and has become an important economic event for China's food industry. As the organizer of the Sugar and Alcoholic Fair, we have been adhering to the principle of serving *enterprises* since the Sugar and Alcoholic Fair was first held in 1955.

After a half century of development, the Sugar and Alcoholic Fair has become well-known in both China and abroad for its display stands covering 60,000 square meters, over 3,000 participants, and a trading volume of over 10 billion yuan. With its wide ranging influence and its increasing attraction, the Fair is commonly recognized among *specialists* in the sugar, food, distillery and brewery industries.

The autumn *phase* of 2011 China National Sugar and Alcoholic Commodities Fair is going to take place in Chengdu. We sincerely invite you to attend the event. Moreover, we hope that this Sugar and Alcoholic Fair will become one of your trading arenas, show platforms, media for information exchange and links for friendships. We believe that our service at various levels will make your visit more valuable.

Do not hesitate to contact us for further information about the Sugar and Alcoholic Fair. Your *inquiry* is welcomed at any time.

Yours sincerely,

○ Sample 2

Dear Sir/Madam,

We hereby sincerely invite you and your company representatives to visit our stand at the Continental Exhibition Center from April 15th to 20th, 2011.

We are one of the manufacturers specialized in sanitary wares, including wash basins, cabinet basins, pedestal basins, bidets, counter basins, decorated ceramics and so on. Our new models offer *superb* design and their new features give them *distinct* advantages over similar products from other manufacturers.

It will be a great pleasure to meet you at the exhibition. We hope to establish a long-term business relationship with your company in the future.

Yours sincerely,

Su Jia

General Manager

Vocabulary

sponsor	/'sponsə/	v. 赞助；发起
respectively	/ri'spektivli/	adv. 分别地；各自地，独自地
enterprise	/'entəpraiz/	n. 企业，事业
specialist	/'speʃəlist/	n. 专家；专门医师
phase	/feiz/	n. 阶段
inquiry	/in'kwaiəri/	n. 调查，咨询
superb	/sju'pə:b/	adj. 极好的，华丽的
distinct	/dis'tiŋkt/	adj. 独特的，清楚的

Notes

1. distillery and brewery industries 酒厂及酿酒工业等行业
2. sanitary ware 卫生洁具

wash basin 洗脸盆	cabinet basin 柜盆
pedestal basin 柱脚脸盆	bidet 坐浴盆
counter basin 台盆	decorated ceramics 陶瓷装饰

Expressions

○ For invitation

We would be happy if…

We request the pleasure of…

Could you join us in…?

We sincerely hope that you can attend…

○ For accepting or rejecting the invitation

We are delighted to accept…

We are sincerely happy to join you…

Thank you for inviting us to…, but I'm afraid I have to say "no" to your kind invitation…

Unfortunately, it will be impossible…

I'm sorry that I can't come to…

I regret to say…

Part III
Practical Writing

Sample Consolidation

♣ Practice 1

Complete the information according to the samples.

Sample 1

Event: _____

Date/Time: _____

Reason: _____

Sample 2

Event: _____

Date/Time: _____

Reason: _____

Grammar Focus

It-cleft Sentences

The sentence pattern of It-cleft sentences with the main function to highlight the emphasized part should be:

It is/was + the emphasized part (stressing the other part of speech except the predicate) + who/ that +...

e.g.: The fair will be held in Guangzhou again.

→ It is in Guangzhou that the fair will be held again.

Notes:

1. If the emphasized part is the interrogative word, the sentence pattern should be: Wh- question word + is/was it + that +...?

e.g.: Where will Tokyo Motor Show (东京车展) be held this year?

→ Where is it that Tokyo Motor Show will be held this year?

2. When the emphasized part is the adverbial clause by *until* and the predicate of the subject sentence is negative, the sentence pattern should be：It is/was + not until + the adverbial clause of time + that + ...

e.g.: We are not able to effect the shipment until the weather becomes better.

→ It is not until the weather becomes better that we are able to effect the shipment.

♣ Practice 2

Choose the best answers to complete the It-cleft sentences below.

1. David said that it was because of his strong interest in accountancy _____ he chose the course at New York University.

    A. that   B. what   C. why   D. how

2. It was nearly a month later _____ I received the manager's reply.

    A. since   B. when   C. as   D. that

3. The Secretary of Commerce said: " _____ we that hope the two sides will cooperate towards peace."

    A. This is   B. There is   C. That is   D. It is

4. It was _____ back to America after the business negotiation.

    A. not until midnight did he go   B. until midnight that he didn't go

    C. not until midnight that he went   D. until midnight when he didn't go

5. When _____ that the general manager left for Japan?

    A. it was   B. was it   C. was that   D. is it

6. It was what he meant, rather than what he said, _____ made me change my company's investment plan.

    A. which   B. as   C. what   D. that

7. It was lack of money, not of effort, _____ defeated their plan.

    A. which   B. as   C. that   D. what

8. It was his nervousness during the interview _____ probably lost him the job.

    A. which   B. since   C. that   D. what

9. It was on October 1st last year _____ the new branch in Sydney was founded.

    A. which   B. when   C. as   D. that

10. _____ is not everybody _____ can finish this program so well.

    A. It, all   B. It, that   C. There, who   D. There, that

♣ Practice 3

Change the following sentences into It-cleft sentences according to the underlined part.

1. <u>What</u> did he tell you at the exhibition yesterday?

2. The general manager <u>didn't</u> turn up <u>until</u> the negotiation began.

3. Jane needs an assistant to deal with her daily business in the office <u>next month</u>.

4. We had a meeting to discuss the new promotion plan <u>in the conference meeting</u>.

5. <u>John</u> reported the annual revenue of the company to the President.

6. He wants to know <u>the reason for the decline in sales this year</u>.

Language Points

♣ Practice 4

Match each word to the correct definition.

1. enterprise	a. to support a person, organization or activity by giving money, encouragement or other help
2. sponsor	b. the power to have an effect on people or things, or a person or thing that is able to do this
3. inquiry	c. company, business
4. influence	d. company that produces goods in large numbers
5. manufacturer	e. the process of asking a question
6. pleasure	f. enjoyment or satisfaction, or something that gives this

1. _____   2. _____   3. _____   4. _____   5. _____   6. _____

♣ Practice 5

Complete the following sentences with the proper form of the words in the box.

receive	patient	favor	invite	vary	design	hold	manage

1. We would like to await good news with _____.

2. Look forward to a _____ reply via return mail.

3. We await the pleasure of _____ your reply at an early date.

4. Our company develops many new _____ and programs this year, and I am sure there must be something attracting your attention.

5. We would like to invite you to attend the Autumn Fair Canton 2011 which will be _____ from Oct. 15th to 21st.

6. You may see _____ kinds of bed sheet sets and comforters made from printing or dyeing fabrics.

7. Our goal is to work hard to make our company become a super global producer of textiles with excellent _____ system, products and services.

8. We sincerely hope that you will accept our _____.

♣ Practice 6

Complete the following sentences in English.

1. _____ (诚挚邀请您参加) to our annual conference to be held on April 12 in New York.

2. _____ (我想知道您是否愿意参加) the company's Christmas party.

3. _____ (非常感谢邀请我们) to the fair next Monday.

4. _____ (盼望你参加) North American International Auto Show (北美底特律车展).

5. _____ (很遗憾不能接受邀请) to see the whole manufacturing process.

Letter Practice

TEMPLATE

Date:

Salutation:

Body:

offer a warm and personal _____

provide _____ about the invitation in terms of "who, what, where, when, why and how"

express the _____ that the invitee will be able to attend and offer the expectation that the event will be a success

♣ Practice 7

Compose an invitation letter with the information given according to the template above.

A. recent technological advances have made our products increasingly affordable to the public

B. The presentation will take place at Shanghai New International Expo Center (上海新国际博览中心)

C. There will also be a reception at 9 o'clock on March 10

D. if you have questions

E. We are looking forward to seeing you on March 10

November 23

Dear Mr. Wilson:

It is with the greatest pleasure that we write to invite you to an exclusive presentation of our new washing-machines. (1) _____ from March 10 to March 12. (2) _____ .

Panasonic is a leading producer of high quality. As you know, (3) _____ . Our new models combine superb quality and sophistication with economy, whose new features give them distinct advantages over similar products from other manufacturers.

(4) _____ . Just call us at (021) 652-87708 (5) _____ .

Sincerely yours,

Dacio Anderson

Dacio Anderson

Marketing Manager

♣ Practice 8

Complete the invitation letter below according to the Chinese in the parentheses.

Houghton Marine Electronic Equipment Co., Ltd.

95 Pine Street

Albany, NY 12204

May 3, 2011

Mr. Jackson

Marketing Manager

Far East Trading Co. Ltd

34 Central Avenue

Albany, NY 12204

Dear Mr. Jackson,

(1) _____ (诚邀您) to our company's tenth annual electronic equipment exhibition. (2) _____ (展览将于5月14日，星期六下午2点举行) at Hilton Hotel.

Currently, our company (3) _____ (开发和推销一系列新电器设备) including electric fans, electric shavers, electric heaters, and air-conditioners (4) _____ (质量好价格合理), which will be presented at the demonstration. (5) _____ (我相信你们会感兴趣).

I am looking forward to a favorable reply.

Yours sincerely,

Angela Papas

Angela Papas

Marketing Manager

◆ Practice 9

Write a reply to the letter of invitation above.

Part IV
Supplementary Reading

Reading One

Dear Darryl Auden,

We are glad to hear via the British Embassy that you would like to bring a trade delegation to China in March on a week-long study tour.

It will be a great pleasure for our company to act as sponsor to your delegation. We will act in cooperation with all the organizations you wish to meet in arranging your program and will try our best to ensure that your visit will be rewarding.

We suggest your delegation arrive on Monday, 6th March. Your program can be designed to cover a week. If this period is not convenient for you, please inform me of the date on which you would prefer to arrive so that we can make the necessary alternative arrangements.

Please furnish us with all the passport details of your delegates so that we can send you formal invitations for the purpose of your visa.

We look forward to the pleasure of welcoming you here.

Yours faithfully,

Reading Two

Dear Sir/Madame,

The High-Level Forum on the theme *China's Economic Development Strategy in the Full Opening-up Era* organized by the Organizing Committee of World Economic Development Declaration (WEDD) will be held from August 18th to 19th, 2011, in order to make Chinese and foreign enterprises well-informed of the world economic situation and China's economic and industrial policies timely, accurately and comprehensively as well as to drive the development of economy. On behalf of the WEDD Organizing Committee, China International Institute of Multinational Corporations hereby invites you to take part in the High-Level Forum on China's Economic Development.

UN officials, Chinese dignitaries and renowned Chinese and foreign economists will be invited and they will offer their practical knowledge and penetrating insights on the issues concerning global economy, China's economic trends in the first half of 2011, monetary policy, policies on foreign investment and foreign trade, industrial development tendency and other related national policies.

A roundtable on Financial Reform and Corporate Financing Strategy will be specially held. Leaders from the People's Bank of China, China Banking Regulatory Commission, China Securities Regulatory Commission and National Development and Reform Commission together with some elites from commercial circles will be invited to attend the meeting.

We value your attention and look forward to your participation in this forum.

Yours sincerely,

Thank-you Letters

Objectives

To be proficient in

◎ understanding the useful words and expressions often used in thank-you letters

◎ writing thank-you letters

◎ using the subordinate conjunctions correctly

Cultural Tips

Thank-you letters are used to express one's gratitude to somebody for their hospitality, help, gifts, recommendation, etc. In the business world, a thank-you letter has become essential if you care about your career. The format of thank-you letters is the same as that of other types of letters. They do not need to be long, but the content should reflect the writer's true and honest feelings and gratitude. When writing thank-you letters, you should describe in detail what you are grateful at the beginning and express your gratitude in an enthusiastic and appreciative way.

Part I
Warm-up Activities

◆ **What should you pay attention to when you write thank-you letters?**

◇ Describe in detail what you are _____ for at the beginning.

◇ Express your _____ in an enthusiastic and appreciative way.

◇ Elaborate on your _____.

◇ Write as soon as possible.

◆ Put the following parts into proper order to make a complete thank-you letter.

A. With the help of your persuasive recommendation, I have already found a satisfactory job in Zhongxing Telecommunication Facilities Company.

B. Sincerely yours, George Brown

C. Thank you very much for the recommendation you provided for me.

D. I will work hard and be worthy of your kindness and assistance.

E. Dear Mr. Henry,

F. My best regards.

Part II
Sample Study

○ Sample 1

Dear Mr. Johnson,

I am writing this letter to thank you for the warm *hospitality* accorded to me and my delegation during our recent visit to your beautiful country. I would also like to thank you for your discussion with me which I found very informative and useful.

During the visit, my *delegation* and I were *overwhelmed* by the *enthusiasm* expressed by your business *representatives*. I sincerely hope we can have more exchanges like this in possible ways to expand our *bilateral* economic and trade relations.

I am looking forward to your early visit to China so that I will be able to pay back some of the hospitality we received during my memorable stay in your beautiful country.

With kind personal regards.

Faithfully yours,
Peter

○ Sample 2

Dear Dr. Hill,

I would like to thank you for interviewing me yesterday for the associate engineer position in your company.

I really enjoyed meeting with members of the staff and learning about the job. The interview strengthened my interest in working for Casey Engineering Systems Inc. It was indeed a pleasure to discuss the opportunities with you.

I strongly feel that I possess the qualities required to be an associate engineer. I believe my education and experience in team work nicely fit in with the job requirements, and I'm certain I could make a significant *contribution* to the firm in time. I eagerly *anticipate* our next meeting. Thank you for the interview and for your time and consideration.

Sincerely yours,
Mike

Vocabulary

hospitality	/ˌhɔspi'tæliti/	n. 好客，殷勤
delegation	/ˌdeli'geiʃən/	n. 代表团；委派，派遣
overwhelm	/ˌəuvə'hwelm/	v. 打翻；覆盖；淹没
enthusiasm	/in'θju:ziæzəm/	n. 热情，热心
representative	/ˌrepri'zentətiv/	n. 代表，代理人
bilateral	/bai'lætərəl/	adj. 存在于双方间的，双边的
contribution	/ˌkɔntri'bju:ʃən/	n. 贡献，捐献，捐助
anticipate	/æn'tisipeit/	v. 预期，期望

Notes

1. expand our bilateral economic and trade relations
   拓展我们双方的经济和贸易关系
2. make a significant contribution to the firm
   为公司做出重要的贡献

Expressions

Please accept my sincere appreciation for…

I am greatly indebted to you for your help.

Thank you for your hospitality/kindness/cooperation.

I'm sincerely grateful for all your help in finding me a place.

Words cannot express how grateful I feel at the moment.

Thank you again for your wonderful hospitality and I am looking forward to seeing you again.

Please accept my most sincere thanks for your timely help, which I will always remember.

I can never forget the attention and kindness shown to us.

Part III
Practical Writing

Sample Consolidation

Practice 1

Complete the information according to the samples.

	Sample 1	Sample 2
Sender:	_____	_____
Recipient:	_____	_____
Event:	_____	_____
Reason:	_____	_____

Grammar Focus

Subordinate Conjunctions

Subordinate conjunctions are words or phrases that connect the main sentence with the subordinate clause to express the complete meaning of the sentence. If the sentence with a subordinate conjunction comes at the beginning, a comma will often follow it. The most common subordinate conjunctions in the English language include the following: *after, although, as far as, as if, as long as, as soon as, as though, because, before, if, in order that, since, so, so that, than, though, unless, until, when, whenever, where, whereas, wherever,* and *while, etc.*

e.g.:

1. If you request any additional information, please do not hesitate to contact me.

2. Because you've done such a good job, I'm giving each of you a 10% bonus.

3. If the quantity of the goods does not conform to what is stipulated in the contract, the importer will refuse to accept the goods.

4. You should send a notice when any change arises in his company.

5. Since the quality of goods is far worse than that of samples, we will have to file a claim if you don't bear all the costs.

6. We suggest that you arrange to establish your L/C right away so that you may receive the first half of the goods at an early date.

Practice 2

Correct the errors in the following sentences.

1. If it is not dealt with well, the seller is unable to get his money.

2. Because there were no ships, so we had to make late shipment.

3. Though I have never read the contract, but I heard of it in my office.

4. No sooner had I finished all the products when the power was suddenly cut off.

5. You'll be late for the weekly conference in your firm until you leave at once.

6. Before you know it, the deal will have been concluded.

7. No matter however carefully he performed the experiment, he had yet not got any satisfactory results.

8. Younger as the boy is, he knows a lot about company management.

9. Not until all the guests came we began to set off for the Bund.

10. Come to my office unless you have time.

♣ Practice 3

Combine the two simple sentences, using the subordinate conjunctions in the parentheses.

1. Please cable us your confirmation. We can pack the goods immediately. (so that)

2. We can establish business relations with you. We shall be pleased. (if)

3. Sales packing can be realized in various forms and with different materials. It is helpful to sales. (as long as)

4. Please use normal containers. You receive special instructions from our agents. (unless)

5. We used carton packing. We had taken measures to prevent them from dampness. (although)

6. We shall advise you by e-mail. The goods are shipped. (as soon as)

Language Points

♣ Practice 4

Match each word to the correct definition.

1. hospitality	a. a strong feeling of excitement and interest in sth. and a desire to become involved in it
2. representative	b. to make sb. want to do sth., especially sth. that involves hard work and effort
3. enthusiasm	c. a person who has been chosen to speak or vote for sb. else or on behalf of a group
4. bilateral	d. a sum of money that is given to a person or an organization in order to help pay for sth.
5. motivate	e. involving two groups of people or two countries
6. contribution	f. friendly and generous behavior towards guests

1. _____   2. _____   3. _____   4. _____   5. _____   6. _____

♣ Practice 5

Complete the following sentences with the proper form of the words in the box.

anticipate	assist	expression	meet	hospitable	confident

1. I will work hard and be worthy of your kindness and _____.

2. Thank you very much for the kind _____ you and your wife showed us during our visit to your country.

3. Thank you for your _____ and your kind regards.

4. I want to say your continued _____ in us is very much appreciated.

5. I enjoyed _____ you and learning more about your research and design work.

6. I'd like to take the opportunity to _____ my sincere gratitude to you.

♣ Practice 6

Complete the following sentences in English.

1. _____ (感谢您昨天面试我) for the associate engineer position in your company.

2. _____ (我代表公司), I would like to thank you for placing an unusually large order with us .

3. _____ (我写信感谢) your kindness to me personally on my visit to your branch in New York early this month.

4. I would like to _____ (借此机会感谢您) for your wonderful hospitality and look forward to seeing you soon.

5. _____ (感谢您费时费力) to keep our customers satisfied.

Letter Practice

TEMPLATE

Date:

Salutation:

Body:

express your _____ for what the recipient has done

give some specific _____ about the event

restate the main idea or show _____

Complimentary Close:

Signature:

♣ Practice 7

Compose a thank-you letter with the given information according to the template above .

A. I look forward to seeing you again

B. I hope to have the opportunity to reciprocate

C. You have a positive genius for organizing

D. Please give my kind regards to your wife

E. I am writing these lines to express my sincere thanks

December 20

Dear Mr. Smith,

(1) _____ for your invitation to a dinner party of your company. I'd like you to know how much your hospitality meant to me. (2) _____. I enjoyed not only the food you prepared, but also the conversation. I shall always remember the time we got together as one of the most valuable moments in my life.

(3) _____. I will feel very honored and pleased if you have time to come to the Christmas party of our company. (4) _____.

Thanks again for your invitation. (5) _____.

Yours sincerely,

Li Ming

Li Ming

🍀 Practice 8

Fill in the blanks to complete the following thank-you letter according to the Chinese in the parentheses.

Dear Mr. Smith,

I would like to thank you most sincerely for (1) _____ (你给我的礼物). Your gift has given me great pleasure, and I will treasure it for the rest of my life.

(2) _____ (我想借此机会感谢您) for all the assistance you have rendered me during my stay in your country. I appreciate being introduced to so many of your friends, who are so kind, helpful and pleasant to get along with. I have learnt a lot from them. (3) _____ (贵公司是参观、学习的理想场所).

I hope that we will continue our friendship, and (4) _____ (建立长期友好关系) between our two companies in the future.

Many thanks and best wishes.

Yours sincerely,

Zhou Hong

🍀 Practice 9

Write a thank-you letter according to the information given below, adding details where necessary.

迈克尔所在的公司与史密斯先生的公司签了一笔大单。请以迈克尔的名义写一封感谢信，感谢他的一贯信任，并表示会珍惜彼此之间的愉快合作。

Part IV
Supplementary Reading

Reading One

Dear Mr. Zhou,

Thanks for the samples of men's jeans you sent to us.

We do appreciate the good quality and fashionable style of your jeans. However, after a careful study of your quotation and the current market, we learn that your price seems to be on the high side. To accept your quotation will leave us with little profit. Thus, we suggest that you give us a 5% discount, which will pave the way for introducing your jeans to our customers.

We look forward to closer cooperation with you in the development of trade between our two companies.

We eagerly hope for your favorable reply.

Yours faithfully,
Stuart Harris

Reading Two

Dear John,

On behalf of my wife and myself, I thank you for the invitation to your institute and for the generous hospitality accorded to us. We enjoyed meeting you and several of your colleagues. The visit was not only a source of pleasure but an opportunity to discuss important matters. Furthermore I gained some fresh ideas.

I am very grateful for the time you spent answering my persistent questions, and for the effort you made, to make our stay in your institute as interesting as possible.

My wife and I are looking forward to the pleasure of playing host to you and your wife in the U.S.A. We would like to have a chance to return your kindness.

With best wishes.

Yours sincerely,
Thomas

Congratulation Letters

Objectives

To be proficient in

◎ understanding the useful words and expressions often used in congratulation letters

◎ writing congratulation letters

◎ dealing with dependent clause fragments correctly

Cultural Tips

Congratulation letters are usually used to express a feeling of sincere blessing and respect, or admiration for somebody's accomplishments. They can be used for the congratulations on engagement, marriage, a newborn baby, birthday, promotion, graduation, etc. Whether writing to a close friend or a distant business associate, any congratulation letter must be sincere and enthusiastic. They may be short, but they should contain personal positive remarks or references.

Part I
Warm-up Activities

◆ **What should you pay attention to if you write a congratulation letter?**

◇ Begin with the expression of _____.

◇ Tell how happy, pleased, proud, or impressed you are, and why.

◇ If appropriate, tell how you learned about _____.

◇ In closing, express _____.

◇ Make your congratulatory letter _____ and _____.

◇ Try to _____ excessive flattery.

◆ **Translate the following congratulation letter into Chinese.**

Dear Edward,

Congratulations on establishing your new company, which means you've finally made your dream come true.

I hope your new company will bring you lots of fortune.

Best wishes.

Yours sincerely,
Shelly

Part II Sample Study

○ Sample 1

Dear Mr. Robert,

I'm so glad to know that you've been promoted to vice president of your company. I would like to *convey* my warm congratulations on your promotion.

Many years of service and experience in *administration* have proved that you are highly qualified and capable of this position, and the utmost contribution you made to your company have at last been rewarded.

Congratulations should also be extended to your *faculty*, for they have the right person as their president.

I wish everything goes well for you in future.

Yours sincerely,
George

○ Sample 2

Dear Jason,

I am much delighted to learn that you have been elected the president of our board. This is a special and happy moment for you and I am very proud of your achievement.

The board plays an *essential* role in our company's management. Managing and *leveraging* such an organization not only poses a

great challenge to you, but also *enhances* your ability *fundamentally* and comprehensively. I believe this position will be a fresh start, and also a chance for you to *embrace* a fuller life and pave the way for a brilliant future career.

Please accept my most sincere congratulations.

Yours sincerely,
Zhang Yang

Vocabulary

convey	/kən'vei/	*v.* 转达，传达 (思想、感情等)
administration	/əd,minis'treiʃən/	*n.* 管理，经营
faculty	/'fækəlti/	*n.* (从事某一职业的) 全体人员
essential	/i'senʃəl/	*adj.* 本质的；基本的；重要的
leverage	/'levəridʒ/	*v.* 衡量；利用
enhance	/in'hæns/	*v.* 提高，增强
fundamentally	/,fʌndə'mentli/	*adv.* 根本上地
embrace	/im'breis/	*v.* 包含

Notes

1. play a ... role in...   在……方面起……的作用
2. pave the way for...   为……铺平道路
3. pose a challenge to...   给……带来挑战

Expressions

I'm writing to you to extend my sincere congratulations on…

I would like to offer my warm congratulations to you on your…

Warm congratulations on your success in / a job well done…

I extend my best wishes for your success and prosperity.

It was a great pleasure to hear of… Congratulations.

On the happy occasion of your company's… anniversary, I write to convey my hearty congratulations.

Part III Practical Writing

Sample Consolidation

♣ Practice 1

Complete the information according to the samples.

	Sample 1	Sample 2
Sender:	_____	_____
Recipient:	_____	_____
Event:	_____	_____
Reason:	_____	_____

Grammar Focus

Dependent Clause Fragments

If a dependent clause exists alone as a sentence, it is called a dependent clause fragment. The dependent clause can not show the complete meaning of a sentence. In order to express the full meaning of a sentence, we should connect the dependent clause to the main clause. Two common methods to correct the dependent clause fragment are as follows:

◇ Connect the dependent clause and the main clause to form a compound sentence. If the dependent clause comes first, a comma will follow to separate the main clause.

◇ Delete the subordinate conjunction in the dependent clause and two simple sentences are formed.

e.g.:

1. Please contact me. If you need more information regarding our products. (dependent clause fragment)

   If you need more information regarding our products, please contact me. (correct)

2. All people coming to our store should be received politely. Because each of them is our potential customer. (dependent clause fragment)

   All people coming to our store should be received politely because each of them is our potential customer. (correct)

3. He did it with confidence. Although he was not experienced in business. (dependent clause fragment)

   He was not experienced in business. He did it with confidence. (correct)

♣ Practice 2

Complete the following sentences in English, using the correct clauses.

1. _____（一旦双方签署合同）, it is legally binding upon both parties.

2. _____ （尽管他最近生意失败了）, he is satisfied with his situation.

3. I'll give you a 2% discount _____ （如果数量超过20吨）.

4. I dare not speak loudly _____ （恐怕打扰正在开会的人）.

5. _____ （无论是谁发的货）, he should be responsible for the mistake.

♣ Practice 3

Correct the dependent clause fragments below.

1. The seller is not permitted to revise his /her offer. <u>Once the firm offer is accepted by the buyer within the validity.</u>

2. It is imperative that references be contacted by either telephone or e-mail. <u>Before you do business with a company.</u>

3. I came to know him. <u>When I went to America as a member of a trade delegation.</u>

4. I will go to your party. <u>Unless something unexpected happens.</u>

5. All companies must conform to local laws. <u>Since they are essentially rooted in the community.</u>

6. We sent the letter by airmail. <u>In order that it might reach them in good time.</u>

7. Please contact the manager after 5:00 p.m. on weekdays. <u>If you have any question or need.</u>

8. We might lodge a claim against them. <u>Because they failed to deliver the goods within the time limit.</u>

Language Points

♣ Practice 4

Match each word to the correct definition.

1. embrace   a. to increase or further improve the quality, value or status of sb./sth.

2. faculty   b. the act of using a lever to open or lift sth.; the force used to do this

3. achievement   c. to put your arms around sb. as a sign of love or friendship

4. leverage   d. a thing that sb. has done successfully, especially by using their own effort and skill

5. enhance   e. all the teachers of a particular university or college

6. challenge   f. a new or difficult task that tests sb.'s ability and skill

1. _____ 2. _____ 3. _____ 4. _____ 5. _____ 6. _____

♣ Practice 5

Complete the following sentences with the proper form of the words in the box.

ship	promote	establish	manage	manufacture	meet

1. It was delightful news for me to learn of the _____ of your own travel agency.

2. We are the _____ of electric shavers.

3. Please accept our sincerest congratulations on your _____.

4. I wish you success in _____ the affairs of the company.

5. 500 TV sets under Contract No. 23 have been ready for _____.

6. I enjoyed _____ with you and I learned a lot about ACM Computer Company.

♣ Practice 6

Complete the following sentences in English.

1. _____ (衷心祝贺) on your appointment to the Board of Electrical Industries Ltd.

2. _____ (请接受我们最衷心的祝贺) on your promotion.

3. _____ (热烈祝贺) on the 5th anniversary of the foundation of your company.

4. Please accept our warmest congratulations on _____ (分店开业) .

5. _____ (致以衷心的祝贺和美好的祝愿) on this milestone in your life.

Letter Practice

TEMPLATE

Date:

Salutation:

Body:

explain _____ you are writing

personalize the _____ that you need to congratulate in _____ positive

way, show best wishes from the _____ or restate the main idea

Complimentary Close:

Signature:

♣ Practice 7

Compose a congratulation letter with the given information according to the template above.

A. Your effort has provided another example

B. I dare say you deserve this honor

C. Please accept my warmest congratulations

D. you have realized your dream

E. I wish you greater success in your future

September 5, 2011

Dear Susan,

　　(1) _____ on your graduation from Oxford University.

　　Last summer, you left for Britain to further your study as soon as you graduated from the Law Department of Fudan University. You were determined to obtain a Master's Degree. I was so glad for your ambition at this time. Now (2) _____ and come back to China.

　　(3) _____ because I knew that you were absorbed in the stacks of papers in the library, and struggled to afford the high tuition fees there. (4) _____ to prove " Where there is a will, there is a way."

　　Since you are so hard-working, you'll surely have a bright future. (5) _____ .

　　Yours sincerely,
　　Della

🍀 Practice 8

You are required to write a congratulation letter according to the information given below.

写信日期：2011年5月18日
　　写信人：Grace
　　收信人：Peter
　　　内容：Peter最近被提升为 ABC贸易公司的总经理，Grace写信表示祝贺。她认为 Peter有能力胜任这项工作，在新的工作岗位上会很出色，最后祝 Peter不断取得进步。

🍀 Practice 9

Write a reply to the above congratulation letter.

Part Ⅳ
Supplementary Reading

Reading One

Dear George,

　　On behalf of the entire team of Electrical Industries Ltd., I would like to heartily congratulate you on your recent graduation from Texas University with a M.A. in Marketing.

　　I was delighted to read about your successful completion of the course in the newspaper. As an intern, a part of our team, you have

contributed immensely to the company. You have a very quick mind for business and a great work ethic, which will help you achieve a wide-open future in your professional life.

The entire company wish you all the best in your future career and life endeavors, whatever they may be.

Yours truly,
David

Reading Two

Dear Mr. Smith,

I was really pleased to learn that you have been selected to be the sales representative of our company in Korea.

Because of our close association with you over the past ten years, we know how well you are qualified for this important office. You earned the promotion through years of hard work and we are delighted to see your true ability win recognition. Although new responsibilities will be put on your shoulder, even bigger and harder, I believe that you will make greater achievements.

Congratulations and best wishes.

Yours sincerely,
Black

Complaint Letters

Objectives

To be proficient in

◎ understanding the useful words and expressions often used in complaint letters

◎ writing complaint letters

◎ using contractions

Cultural Tips

A letter of complaint requests compensation for defective or damaged goods or for poor services. It usually consists of the following parts:

◇ Background: describing the situation

◇ Problem: explaining cause and effect

◇ Solution: stating exactly what you want to be done about the problem

◇ Warning: introducing actions to take if the problem is not solved

◇ Closing: ending with a desire to solve the problem

An effective complaint letter should contain the necessary facts. It must be short, clear, and friendly.

Part I
Warm-up Activities

◆ **What key elements should be included if you write a letter of complaint?**

Key Elements

COMPLAINT

TO:
WHOSE FAULT:
DESIRED OUTCOME:

COMPLAINANT:

_____

_____

_____

_____

◆ **Write a letter of complaint according to the following situation.**

You ordered a shirt from Wind Company online two weeks ago. But unfortunately, they sent you the wrong size. Write an e-mail to ask the company to send you the right-sized shirt and reimburse the fee for sending the wrong shirt back to them.

Complaint to: _____

Complaint for: _____

Ask for: _____

Part II
Sample Study

○ **Sample 1**

Dear Sir or Madam,

I am writing to inform you that the goods your company shipped for us have not been correctly supplied. On 1 November we *consigned* 12,000 super long-life batteries to your company for shipment. The consignment arrived yesterday, but it only contained 10,000 batteries.

This error has put our firm in a difficult position, as we had to make some *emergency* purchases to fulfill our *commitment* to all our customers. This has caused us *considerable inconvenience*.

I am writing to ask you to make up the *shortfall* immediately and to ensure that such errors do not happen again. Otherwise, we may have to look elsewhere for shipment.

I look forward to hearing from you.

Yours faithfully,

Jack Walters

Purchasing Officer

○ Sample 2

Dear Sir or Madam,

I am writing to let you know the *deplorable* attitude of one of your staff members. I received my telephone bill for the *previous* month from you and thought there were some errors in calculation: I had been overcharged for two overseas calls. However, when I called your complaints department, the girl who answered my phone was very rude. For one thing, she interrupted me frequently; for another, she even said that it was my own fault.

Needless to say, such a way of dealing with customers is unacceptable. I would like to suggest that the girl in question should be *disciplined*, and instructed to deal with clients in the correct way. Additionally, I hope she can make a formal apology to me.

An early response would be appreciated.

Sincerely yours,
Mary

Vocabulary

consign	/kən'sain/	v. 托运，发送，把……委托给
emergency	/i'məːdʒənsi/	n. 紧急情况，突发事件，急诊
commitment	/kə'mitmənt/	n. 托付，承诺，保证
considerable	/kən'sidərəbl/	adj. 相当大的，重要的　n. 大量
inconvenience	/ˌinkən'viːnjəns/	n. 不便，麻烦
shortfall	/'ʃɔːtfɔːl/	n. 差额，赤字
deplorable	/di'plɔːrəbl/	adj. 可悲的，可怜的，糟糕的
previous	/'priːvjəs/	adj. 先的，前的，以前的
disciplined	/'disiplind/	adj. 受过训练的，遵守纪律的

Notes

1. make up the shortfall	弥补损失
2. complaints department	投诉部；客服部
3. needless to say	很显然，不用说，毋庸置疑

Expressions

For describing complaints

We regret to have to inform you that… arrived in an unsatisfactory condition.

Our customers complain that the goods are considerably inferior in quality to the samples.

We are surprised and disappointed at their quality.

We reserve our right to lodge a claim against you.

For presenting solutions

We request that you send five new pieces as replacements as soon as possible.

If you can not accept, I'm afraid we shall have to return them for replacement.

A quick refund will be highly appreciated.

Part III Practical Writing

Sample Consolidation

Practice 1

Complete the information according to the samples.

	Sample 1	Sample 2
Background:	__________	__________
Problem:	__________	__________
Solution:	__________	__________
Warning:	__________	__________
Closing:	__________	__________

Grammar Focus

Contractions

A contraction refers to shortened form of two or more words by omitting or combining some sounds instead of the full form in spoken English.

e.g.:

Informal: We're interested in upgrading our computer system.

Formal: We are interested in upgrading our computer system.

Practice 2

Fill in the following blanks with the contractions.

1. _____ (He is) living at some place in East Africa.
2. I (do not) _____ think there is any petrol in the tank.
3. _____ (Did not) you put some logos on the packages?
4. I _____ (have not) taken much money with me.
5. _____ (There is) only a little time left.
6. _____ (I will) deliver the goods you ordered tonight.
7. Unless _____ (you are) paying by credit card, please pay in cash.
8. _____ (It is) doubtful whether _____ (we will) be able to come to your company's 5th anniversary party.
9. He _____ (was not) sure whether he ought to establish new company or not.
10. I wish you _____ (would not) look down on this kind of work.

Language Points

Practice 3

Match each word to the correct definition.

1. commitment
2. inconvenience
3. disciplined
4. considerable
5. emergency
6. consign

a. serious event or situation needing prompt action
b. great, much, important
c. promise, pledge, undertaking
d. trained and controlled (mind and character)
e. to send goods for delivery
f. cause or instance of discomfort or trouble

1. ____ 2. ____ 3. ____ 4. ____ 5. ____ 6. ____

Practice 4

Complete the following sentences with the proper form of the words in the box.

| equip | occasion | buy | wonder | leave | perform | solve | concentrate |

1. Obviously, nuclear power can never be the only _____ to the energy crisis.
2. The young man did not have enough money; otherwise he would have _____ a more expensive watch.
3. The boss gave him a raise in his salary because of his excellent _____ at work.
4. This hospital, which is _____ with modern facilities, is one of the best in our country.
5. It's really _____ to see you here again in Beijing.
6. Successful companies _____ more on selling their products to their existing customers than to their new ones.

7. With such a short time _____, it's impossible for us to finish this complicated experiment.

8. Since we work in different sections of the company, we see each other only _____.

Practice 5

Complete the following sentences in English.

1. The report indicates that _____ (此损失是由于包装袋不合标准所致), for which the suppliers are responsible.

2. We enclose Survey Report No. FH2352 and _____ (烦请早日解决赔偿事宜).

3. We regret having to inform you that the cotton goods arrived in such an unsatisfactory condition that _____ (只好向贵方提出索赔).

4. _____ (我们验货时发现) that 150 cameras, in 2 cases, are severely damaged.

5. We expect you _____ (对此事给予及时关注).

6. We have received your goods yesterday. But I'm sorry to say _____ (其质量不太令人满意).

Letter Practice

TEMPLATE

Date:

Salutation:

Body:

state the _____ you have with the product, the work or the service and why

present the _____ to the problem

hope to get the _____ soon

Complimentary Close:

Signature:

Practice 6

Compose a letter of complaint with the information given according to the template above.

A. there must be some mistakes in your making up the order

B. we are prepared to allow the stated time for delivery

C. They certainly do not match the samples you sent us

D. supplied for our order of 20th February

E. we shall have to ask you to cancel our order

Dear Sir:

After carefully examining the curtain materials (1) _____ , we must express surprise and disappointment at their quality. (2) _____ . Some of them are so poor that we can't help feeling (3) _____ . The materials are quite unsuited to the needs of our customers and we have no choice but to ask you to take them back and replace them with materials of the quality ordered. If this is not possible, then I am afraid (4) _____ .We have no wish to embarrass you and if you can replace the materials, (5) _____ .

Sincerely yours,

Black

Marketing Manager

♣ Practice 7

Read the information below and complete the letter of complaint, adding details where necessary.

你是某银行信用卡的老顾客，且无不良记录；现因对客服态度不满写信投诉，希望得到快速满意的答复。

Dear Sir,

(1) _____ for the past ten years and (2) _____ . However, when I sought a temporary increase in my credit limit yesterday, I was told by your customer service officer that he would have to check the authenticity of my application by calling up my company to verify. (3)_____ . Although you have the duty to check all applications, (4) _____ .

(5) _____ .

Yours sincerely,

♣ Practice 8

Write a reply to the letter of complaint above.

Part IV
Supplementary Reading

Reading One

Dear Sir or Madam,

I am happy that the refrigerator we ordered last week has arrived on time. Unfortunately, we have found something wrong with the refrigeration facilities.

After several days' use, we found that food stored in the refrigerating compartment turned bad quickly. When we measured the temperature, we were surprised to find it was around 15℃, far above the standard temperature range of 0℃ to 9℃.

This problem has affected our life. Could you please let me know whether or not you can send a repairman as soon as possible? I hope that my problem will get your kind consideration.

Yours faithfully,

Yang Li

Reading Two

Dear Sir:

With reference to our order No. W98, the 120 computer sets supplied to the above order were delivered the day before yesterday, but we regret that 20 sets were badly damaged.

The packages containing the computer sets appeared to be in good condition and we accepted and signed for them without question. We unpacked the computer sets with care and can only assume that damage must be due to careless handling at some stage prior to packing.

We shall be glad if you will replace all 20 sets as soon as possible. Meanwhile, we have put the damaged computer sets aside in case you need them to support a claim against your suppliers for compensation.

Yours sincerely,

Li Ming

Apology Letters

Objectives

To be proficient in

◎ understanding the useful words and expressions often used in apology letters

◎ writing apology letters

◎ using consistency in pronouns

Cultural Tips

Business apology letters are relatively formal and usually include the following contents: first making an apology; then giving an adequate and convincing explanation of a situation that requires an apology; finally sincerely hoping the other party will accept the apology. The tone should be honest and friendly.

Part I Warm-up Activities

◆ **Work in pairs and fill in the blanks.**

What are the basic elements of apology letters?

◇ Apologize to the _____

◇ Explain the _____ for apology

◇ Ask the receiver to accept your _____ sincerely

◆ **Write the reasons for apologizing and the solution according to the apology letter below.**

1836 Price Road

Rockford, IL6233

March 26, 2010

Mr. Rober Varadi

365 Krogstad Street

Loves Park, IL6233

Dear Mr. Varadi:

I would like to apologize for the mix-up on your last order. Our new sales person was not familiar with your systems. We have corrected your order and shipped it out this afternoon. We have applied a 8% discount on your order, and again apologize for any inconvenience this may have caused you.

Yours sincerely,

Wang Haipeng

Customer Service Manager

Apologize for: _____

The solution: _____

Part Ⅱ
Sample Study

○ Sample 1

April 13, 2011

Dear Mr. Bean,

We *regret* to say that we cannot punctually send you the *catalogue* and price list which you asked for in your letter of April 12. These supplies will not be expected from the *printer* until next Monday because there is something wrong with the machines. As soon as we receive them, we will send you without any delay.

We are pleased to have *finalized* this business with you. Please be assured that our products are the finest on the market and the price we offered is the most favorable among the *competitors*. We expect this delay will not influence our cooperation.

I'll be grateful if you can receive our sincere apology.

Yours faithfully,

David Law

David Law

○ Sample 2

December 21, 2011

Dear Mr. Joe,

I am, indeed, grateful for your letter of December 17. I must *apologize* for my *delay* in answering the letter. When your letter arrived, I was in Japan on business. Therefore my secretary could not forward it to me during my *absence*. The  first thing I did when I came back was to write these few lines to you to express my deep regret.

Attached please find the beautiful cards I bought during my trip. I hope you will like it. Apologize again for the late reply to your letter.

Sincerely yours,

Tom

 Vocabulary

regret	/riˈgret/	v. 懊悔，惋惜，遗憾
catalogue	/ˈkætəlɔg/	n. 目录，一览表
printer	/ˈprintə/	n. 印刷厂；印刷工人；印刷机
finalize	/ˈfainəlaiz/	v. 完成，达成
competitor	/kəmˈpetitə/	n. 竞争者，对手，参赛者
apologize	/əˈpɔlədʒaiz/	v. 道歉，认错，愧悔
delay	/diˈlei/	n. 耽搁，延迟
absence	/ˈæbsəns/	n. 缺席，离开

 Expressions

I'm terribly/awfully/very sorry for…

I'm sorry/regret/that…

I must apologize for…

Please accept my apology for…

I should be much obliged if you will excuse me.

I hope you will accept my apology.

Part III Practical Writing

Sample Consolidation

♣ Practice 1

Complete the information according to the samples.

	Sample 1	Sample 2
The person who apologizes:	_____	_____
The person accepting apology:	_____	_____
Event:	_____	_____
Date/Time:	_____	_____
Reason:	_____	_____

Grammar Focus

Consistency in Pronouns

The pronouns in English can be divided into personal pronouns, possessive pronouns, reflexive pronouns, demonstrative pronouns, indefinite pronouns, etc. The pronouns must conform to their person, number, gender and case.

1. Consistency in nominatives, accusatives, possessive pronouns and reflexive pronouns.

▶ The nominatives are consistent with their accusatives.

e.g.: We are confident that the goods you are offering us are excellent.

▶ The nominatives are consistent with their possessive pronouns.

e.g.: Both my brother and I like our own jobs respectively.

▶ The nominatives are consistent with their reflexive pronouns.

e.g.: Our clients themselves purchased some tons a few weeks ago from our stock.

2. Consistency in pronouns and verbs.

e.g.: He refers to your offer of March 2 for 1,000 pieces of the subject articles.

3. Consistency in pronouns and their antecedents.

A pronoun which usually refers to the thing or person mentioned in the previous part of a sentence (its antecedent), singular or plural, must be consistent with its antecedent.

e.g.: Ms. Andrew decides to make a tight budget this year, and she hopes to receive the support from the manager of the company.

Notes:

If the subject is singular, followed by *with, together with, as well as, as much as, no less than, more than,* etc., the verb must remain singular.

e.g.: An expert, together with some assistants, was sent to help with this work.

4. Consistency in indefinite nouns.

▶ If the singular indefinite nouns such as *everything, anything, nothing, everyone, someone, no one, somebody, nobody, anyone, each,* etc. are used as the subjects, the verbs should also be singular.

e.g.: Please tell the manager if someone comes here.

▶ If the plural indefinite nouns such as *many, both, several, few* etc. are used as subjects, the verbs should also be plural.

e.g.: Few are welcome to attend the business meeting.

▶ Some pronouns such as *some, all, none, any* and so on, can be used either as singular or plural according to the context.

e.g.: Please look at the old office equipment. Some is to be replaced.

Some of them have agreed to deliver the goods to the port.

✤ Practice 2

Choose the best answer.

1. We _____ pleased to say how pleased we _____ to receive your order of June 8.

   A. are, are   B. are, were   C. were, are   D. were, were

2. All of them enjoyed _____ at the 5th anniversary party of Tom's company.

   A. them   B. themselves   C. themselves   D. himself

3. With this letter, we confirm _____ of the bed sheets at the price stated in your e-mail yesterday.

   A. our supply   B. supply   C. the supply   D. ourselves

4. Now that everything _____ made clear, we should dispatch next week by rail.

   A. are   B. were   C. x   D. is

5. She is the only one of the girls in our class who _____ fond of doing business.

   A. is   B. are   C. be   D. has been

6. Do you really believe that Mr. White has blamed us for the error in shipping, especially _____ ?

   A. you and me   B. I and you   C. you and I   D. you and we

7. The importer will submit references if these _____ given in the preliminary negotiations.

   A. are not   B. was not   C. has not been   D. did not

8. In the case, the buyer _____ cancel the contract.

   A. could   B. have the right to

   C. may have to   D. reserves the right to

9. His earliest sales performance is excellent, but his latest one is _____.

    A. something   B. everything   C. anything   D. nothing

10. He _____ your terms satisfactory and now sends you our order for 3 sets of generators.

    A. find   B. found   C. finds   D. had found

Practice 3

Correct the errors in the following sentences.

1. Ours company exports textile products to many countries.

2. Companies must try themselves best to improve the quality of products and services to meet the needs of the customers.

3. John opened him own trade company in 2006.

4. She must make an apology for hers mistakes.

5. Nobody here are against the new proposal of establishing a trade relationship with Sunshine Flavors Ltd.

6. By the time Martin and myself got to the airport, the plane had taken off.

Language Points

Practice 4

Match each word to the correct definition.

1. apologize   a. to make (someone or something) late or slow

2. attend   b. to express regret for something that one has done wrong

3. delay   c. to cause (someone) to believe firmly in the truth of something

4. regret   d. to be present at (an event, meeting, or function)

5. convince   e. to feel sad, repentant, or disappointed over something

1. _____   2. _____   3. _____   4. _____   5. _____

Practice 5

Complete the following sentences with the proper form of the words in the box.

postpone	convince	attend	apology	absent	regret

1. I'm terribly sorry that the dinner we have planned for Nov. 12 must be _____.

2. I must _____ that I failed to see you off at the airport.

3. I _____ not being able to answer your letter at an early date.

4. Please excuse my _____ from your anniversary party.

5. The _____ of the Spring Fair Canton 2010 is considerable.

6. I am writing to express my heartfelt thanks and deep regret and I hope you will be _____ that the delay was excusable.

Practice 6

Complete the following sentences in English.

1. _____ (很抱歉让您久等了), and let's begin our business negotiation immediately.

2. _____ (我感到非常抱歉) for being late for the meeting held by your company last Monday.

3. I must apologize that _____ (下周二不能参加展销会).

4. _____ (写信向您道歉) for my delay in answering your letter.

5. _____ (请原谅我的粗心) for damaging your glass products.

6. _____ (让您误了航班是我的过错), please accept my sincere apology.

TEMPLATE

Date:

Salutation:

Body:

offer a sincere and personal _____

provide a convincing _____ about the apology

express the apology again and hope they can _____ the apology

Complimentary Close:

Signature:

Practice 7

Compose a letter of apology with the given information according to the template above.

A. we have to put off our talk

B. talk about our business this Thursday

C. I can't meet you until next Monday

D. express my sincere apology to you

E. this change will not influence your work

September 6, 2011

Mr. James
73 King Street
Wara Wong 2805

Dear Mr. James:

First I want to (1) _____ . We had arranged to (2) _____ , but my manager arranged me to go to Beijing on business with him and (3) _____ . I am so sorry that (4) _____ . I hope (5) _____ .

Apologize sincerely again.

Sincerely yours,

Hank Gruff

Hank Gruff

Sales Manager

🌸 Practice 8

Read the information below and complete the letter of apology below.

Modern Mechanics Equipment Co. Ltd. will hold its sixth anniversary party on Saturday, June 24, at 2 o'clock at Holiday Inn. You (Li Gang) has to attend an important meeting in Shanghai and can't attend it, so you apologize to Mr. White, the sales manager of the company, for your absence.

June 21, 2011

Mr. White

(1) _____

Modern Mechanics Equipment Co. Ltd.

126 Maple Street

Albany, LL 12350

Dear Mr. White,

(2) _____ that I can't attend your company's sixth anniversary party, (3) _____ at Holiday Inn because (4) _____ .

(5) _____ . I wish your anniversary party a great success.

Yours sincerely,

Li Gang

Marketing Manager

🍀 Practice 9

Write a letter of apology according to the information below.

Brown被任命为公司新的市场部经理，邀请人事部经理Lucy参加11月6日晚上7点在家举行的庆祝晚宴。但公司的重要客户Mary因有急事需赶回纽约，总经理临时安排Lucy去机场送行，故不能参加。请以Lucy的名义向Brown写封道歉信。

Part IV
Supplementary Reading

Reading One

March 19, 2011

Mr. Steve Whitman
225 Gilbert Road
Loves Park, IL 61111

Dear Mr. Whitman:

I would like to apologize to you for not attending the committee meeting yesterday morning.

In fact, because I was very busy all day, the meeting slipped my mind completely and I did not remember it until last night. I am very sorry for such a poor performance at the committee's first meeting. I assure you that this won't happen again.

Again I apologize for my absence at the meeting and I should be much obliged if you can forgive me.

Yours sincerely,
Gerald Belknap
Gerald Belknap
Customer Service Manager

Reading Two

Dear Ms. Liu:

I was very concerned when I received yesterday's letter. I'm sorry for your complaint that the central heating system in your new house has not been completed by the promised date.

In reference to our earlier letters, I found that I had made a mistake in the completion date. I realize the inconvenience that our ignorance must be causing you and will do my best to avoid any further delay. I have already given instructions that the work should be prioritised and that the engineers have to work overtime. The installation will be completed by next weekend.

I hope you will accept my sincere apology.

Yours faithfully,
Roy
Chief Engineer

Unit 3

In-house Correspondence
事务处理

Notices

Objectives

To be proficient in
○ understanding the useful words and expressions often used in notices
○ writing notices
○ dealing with unnecessary words correctly

Cultural Tips

Generally, there are two types of notices: notices not only are the messages circulated to those who are concerned, but also refer to the announcements that are placed on the bulletin boards or to be published in the press.

In addition to the rules of good business writing, you should keep your notices as brief as possible, only including what is essential. Your heading or opening should be eye-catching and stimulating.

 Part I
Warm-up Activities

◆ **Work in pairs and complete the key elements included in a notice.**

◇ A _____ briefly stating the subject matter of or just the subject _____
◇ The _____ of the message
◇ A _____ of the person or department responsible for issuing the notice
◇ The _____ of issuing the notice

教师会议

日期：11月03日
时间：上午11：30
地点：协会3楼教室
（永乐路21号3楼）

◆ **Read the notice below and fill in the blanks.**

> ### Notice
>
> *There will be a world trade seminar:*
>
> *"New Trade Policy"*
>
> 9:00 a.m. Monday, March 21
>
> Conference Room, Third Floor, 501 Elm Street
>
> Admission Fee: $ 5
>
> Call (417)528-6348 for more information.

◇ Event: _____

◇ Time: _____

◇ Place: _____

◇ Contact number: _____

Part II
Sample Study

Sample 1

> ### Notice
>
> We have opened a new shop in the eastern *district*, for the *convenience* of customers, who wish to obtain *fashionable* clothing of the most *reliable* quality at reasonable prices.
>
> Welcome to our shop.
>
>
>
> Easter Dress Shop
>
> June 12, 2011

Sample 2

> ### New Appointment Notice
>
> **To:** all customers
>
> We wish to *notify* that Mr. Tony Smart, who has been our sales representative in China for the past five years, has left our company. We have *appointed* Mr. Fred Whitman in his place and he has *authority* to take orders or collect accounts on our behalf now.
>
>
>
> Red Maple Textile Trade Company
>
> February 18, 2011

Vocabulary

district	/'distrikt/	n. 地区，区域，行政区
convenience	/kən'viːnjəns/	n. 方便，便利
fashionable	/'fæʃənəbl/	adj. 流行的，符合时尚的，时髦的
reliable	/ri'laiəbl/	adj. 可靠的，可信赖的
notify	/'nəutifai/	v. 通知，告知，报告
appoint	/ə'pɔint/	v. 任命，委派
authority	/ɔː'θɔriti/	n. 权力，职权；官方

Expressions

Attention please…

We are pleased to announce you that…

I have the honor to inform you that…

We hereby inform you that…

We have the pleasure of announcing that…

Part Ⅲ
Practical Writing

Sample Consolidation

♣ Practice 1

Complete the information according to the samples.

	Sample 1	Sample 2
The person who notify:	_____	_____
The person who was notified:	_____	_____
Event:	_____	_____
Date/Time:	_____	_____

Grammar Focus

Unnecessary Words

Unnecessary words, or redundancies, refer to some words whose meaning is repeated, which make sentences wordy, redundant and even incorrect. By removing these words, sentences can be accurate and concise.

e.g.:

We have begun to export our machines abroad.

We have begun to export our machines.

Note:

The word "export" in the sentence refers to "send goods abroad", so "abroad" at the end of the sentence is an unnecessary duplication.

The following are some verbose words and their shortened form for comparison:

Verbose Form	Shortened Form
a large number of	many
at all times	always
at the present time	now
be able to	can
big in size	big
in the near future	soon
by means of	by
due to the fact that	because
during the time that	while
for the reason that	because
for the purpose of	for
in the event that	if
as a matter of fact	in fact

♣ Practice 2

Choose the best answer to complete the sentences below.

1. _____ (For the reason that/Because) I had to go to Korea on business, I can't attend your company's 5th anniversary party.

2. _____ (If/Unless) you still didn't ship the goods we ordered, we would cancel the order.

3. _____ (During the time that/While) she was on business in Paris, she met her best friend Lisa.

4. He _____ (always/at all times) works at opening another sub-company in China.

5. We are enclosing a copy of our catalogue including all the articles available _____ (at the present time/now).

6. It is important for _____ (many/a large member of) companies to purchase supplies at economic prices.

7. My friend is going to be promoted as Marketing Manager of a large company _____ (soon/in the near future).

8. Without his help, I _____ (am able to/can) hardly handle the complaints of delaying in shipping.

♣ Practice 3

Correct the following unnecessary words in the underlined part.

1. Our company imports industrial products, chemicals, medicines, <u>and etc.</u>

2. <u>The reason why</u> I can't attend your party is <u>because</u> I have to meet an important customer at the airport.

3. Joe opened a trade company <u>in the year of 2008.</u>

4. <u>Without a shadow of doubt</u> we must make an apology for our mistakes.

5. <u>As a matter of fact</u> it was Mike who became the manager.

6. <u>At this point of time</u> Sandy has not reached her home.

Language Points

♣ Practice 4

Match each word to the correct definition.

1. convenience	a. the state of being able to proceed with something with little effort or difficulty
2. notify	b. typical of a class, group, or body of opinion
3. representative	c. to assign a job or role to (someone)
4. appoint	d. a person or organization that buys goods or services from a store or business
5. cooperation	e. to inform (someone) of something, typically in a formal or official manner
6. customer	f. the process of working together to the same end

1. _____   2. _____   3. _____   4. _____   5. _____   6. _____

♣ Practice 5

Complete the following sentences with the proper form of the words in the box.

attention	arrange	inform	require	résumé	notify

1. We must _____ you that you should attend a press conference at 4 o'clock tomorrow afternoon.

2. All the managers are _____ to meet in Room 501.

3. _____, please. We have opened a chain store at the address above.

4. Our company will _____ a New Year's party in the biggest meeting room.

5. We _____ you that our company will attend the Autumn Fair Canton 2011 held by your company.

6. Tomorrow being National Day, there will be no work for seven days, and it will be _____ on Oct. 8.

Practice 6

Complete the following sentences in English.

1. _____ (很荣幸通知您) that we have agreed to establish a trade relationship with your company.

2. _____ (很高兴通知大家) that the company's Christmas party will be held today at 7:00 p.m. in the dancing hall.

3. _____ (现通知) that tomorrow's meeting will be postponed until next Monday.

4. _____ (谨告知本公司顾客) that the two firms above have been amalgamated under the title of P & R this day.

5. _____ (谨宣告) that a five-day-long business visit to Beijing has been arranged from June 7 to June 11.

Letter Practice

TEMPLATE

Notice

Body:

use the words "*Attention, please!*" or "*This is to inform you...*" to attract the _____ of others

provide _____ about notice in terms of event or reason

Notice Maker:

Date:

Practice 7

Compose a notice with the given information according to the template above.

A. there will be no work for seven days

B. The bus will leave at 7:00 a.m. sharp

C. All members are required

D. arrange a visit

E. Please collect at the company gate

Notice

Tomorrow is Labor Day, therefore (1) _____ .

The Marketing Department will (2) _____ to Shanghai New International Expo Center (上海新国际博览中心) from May 1st (Monday) to May 5th(Friday). (3) ___ _____ to take part in this activity. (4) _____ at 7:00 a.m. on May 1st (Monday).

(5) _____ .

The Marketing Department

April 30, 2011

Practice 8

Complete the notice below according to the Chinese in the parentheses.

Lay Off Notice

Dear Employees,

Because of the recent recession, (1) _____ (我们公司的订单大幅下降).

Unfortunately, we have to (2) _____ (解雇40%的流水线工人).Your last day of work will be Saturday. Please pick up your paycheck at the payroll office on that day.

(3) _____ (非常抱歉) to have lay you off at this time. If you have any comment about this situation, please send it to us by using the attached form.

(4) _____ (感谢你们的付出) at Qintong Automatic Control Equipment Co., Ltd.

Manager

Sept. 2, 2011

Practice 9

Write a notice according to the information below.

由于总经理出差，原定于 5 月 8 日（星期三）上午 8:00 在 505 会议室举行的管理会议，推迟到 5 月 10 日（星期五）举行。

Part IV
Supplementary Reading

Reading One

Notice

To: All Managers

The next monthly management meeting will be held at 10:00 a.m. on Monday, April 8, in

Conference Room 202.

The agenda for the meeting is as follows:

◇ Purchase of new office computers

◇ Budgetary control

If there is any other item you would like to place on the agenda, let me know by e-mail by the end of this week.

Thank you.

John Du

Secretary to General Manager

March 20, 2011

Reading Two

Staff Recruitment Notice

Dear Mr. Li:

After preliminary examination, you are the successful applicant for the salesperson position in Modern Technology Company. We sincerely welcome you to join our ranks. Please proceed with the following information.

1. Check-in time: March 5 (Monday) 8:00 a.m.

2. Location: Personnel Department

3. Data necessary to carry:

◇ recruitment notice

◇ identity card

◇ the original academic certificate of highest degree

◇ certificates (or appointment cards)

◇ medical examination certificate

According to company rules, the new employees in the company must first have a trial of 3 months in probation period. Salary of this period is ￥1500 per month.

If you need further information about the mentioned issues, please contact Personnel Department of the company:

Tel.: 0731-88593501

Daniel Liu

Personnel Department Manager

Modern Technology Company

March 2, 2011

E-mails

Objectives

To be proficient in

◎ understanding useful words and expressions often used in e-mails

◎ writing an e-mail

◎ using passive voice

Cultural Tips

An e-mail is a kind of letter which is sent to others by the Internet. It has some advantages such as arriving instantly, being brief and cheap.

In general, an e-mail has two main parts: heading and body. The heading includes the following content: sender, receiver, date, subject and attachment. The layout of the body is like that of a private letter, including heading, salutation, body, complimentary close and signature. But sometimes it just has the parts of salutation and body, while complimentary close and signature are omitted.

Part I
Warm-up Activities

◆ **Write out the necessary elements involved in an e-mail.**

_____

_____

_____

_____

◆ **Fill out the following e-mail according to the information given.**

From: Merry Granger

To: Mr. Lee

Information Source: address obtained from *China Daily*

Purposes:

to establish business relationship

to know about textile industrial products

to get all necessary information about products

From: _____

To : _____

Subject: _____

Dear Mr. Lee,

We have obtained your address from _____ and are writing for the establishment of business relationship with you.

We are well connected with all the major dealers here of _____, and feel sure we can sell large quantities of soft goods if we get your offers at competitive prices.

It is grateful if you can provide us all necessary _____ we required.

Yours sincerely,

Merry Granger

Part II Sample Study

○ Sample 1

To: man@153.com

Subject: Self-introduction

Cc: rochina@hotmail.com

Bcc: apple.lee@yahoo.com

From: greatglovesco@127.net

Date: Monday, January 2, 2012 10:32 AM

Dear Sir or Madam,

We got your name and address from the ABC Commercial Office, and we know that your firm is of good standing and *reliability* in India. We wish to *inform* you that we specialize in the trade of gloves, and shall be pleased to *establish* trade relationship with you.

Our company is one of the leading dealers in gloves in North China. Our customers are very interested in your gloves and hope to receive more information about the *quality*. We believe there is a great market *prospect* of glove sales here. If you can supply goods of the type and quality we required, we may place regular orders for large *quantities*. Before we place a firm order, we hope we can receive your samples, ten for men and ten for women.

We hope this will be a good start for a long and *profitable* business relationship and look forward to your early reply.

Yours sincerely,

Li Min

Li Min

○ Sample 2

From: Tom<Tom6889@aat.co.jp>
To: Henry <Henry999@126.net>
Subject: Meeting

Henry,

I received your voice message regarding the subject. I'm wondering if we need to *arrange* a meeting to discuss more details. Also, the following *items* are expected to be prepared or collected in advance:

◇ catalogue and price list of the products
◇ samples and feedback information
◇ market research report
◇ market forecast report
◇ related information of our *potential* competitors
◇ relevant contracts and documents

Please inform me an exact meeting time at the earliest time once everything is prepared.

Tom

Vocabulary

reliability	/riˌlaiəˈbiləti/	*n.* 可靠性
inform	/inˈfɔːm/	*v.* 通知，告诉
establish	/isˈtæbliʃ/	*v.* 建立，创办
quality	/ˈkwɔliti/	*n.* 质量，品质；特性

prospect	/'prɔspekt/	*n.* 前景，预期；潜在顾客
quantity	/'kwɔntiti/	*n.* 量，数量，大量
profitable	/'prɔfitəbl/	*adj.* 有利可图的，赚钱的
arrange	/ə'reindʒ/	*v.* 安排，整理
item	/'aitəm/	*n.* 条款，项目
potential	/pə'tenʃəl/	*adj.* 可能的，潜在的

Notes

1. reliability

    high reliability 高可靠性；高可靠度

    reliability analysis 可靠性分析

    reliability design 可靠性设计

    reliability theory 可靠性理论

    system reliability 系统可靠性

2. specialize in 专门研究……

We specialize in the development of plastic packing materials.

我们专营塑料包装材料的开发。

Technical writers specialize in producing materials such as instruction manuals and software documentation.

技术作家专门负责创作材料如说明书、软件文档等。

3. establish

establish a business relationship with 建立业务关系

establish a business 创业；设立商店

We write you with a view to establish trade relations.

我们写这封信是为了要和你方建立业务关系。

4. quality

high quality 高品质

product quality 产品质量

quality control 质量控制

quality management 质量管理

quality first 质量第一

Could you recommend a pair of good quality?

你能推荐一双质量好的吗?

Strict quality control ensures the higher quality of products.

严格的质量管理是产品优质的保证。

It is not quality management but process management—the process of improvement.

它不是质量管理，而是过程管理——改进的过程。

5. prospect

market prospect　市场前景

bright prospect　光明的前景

at the prospect of　期待着（想到要）

in prospect of　期待，有希望

We foresee a bright prospect for your products in our market.

我们预见贵方产品在我方具有广阔的市场。

Most are thrilled by the idea of export growth, but cower at the prospect of great imports.

大多数人对出口增长感到兴奋，但是担忧未来进口的大量增长。

In prospect of increase in demand, we should operate at full capacity.

预计需求会有很大增长，我们应该开足马力生产。

We are very optimistic in the prospect of China's growing economy.

我们对于中国经济增长前景十分乐观。

6. quantity

large quantity 大量；大数量

in quantity 大量

A futures contract is an agreement to buy or sell a quantity of a product at a set price and date in the future.

期货合同是按照商定的价格和日期在将来某时买卖一定数量产品的协议。

If you order in large quantity, we will give you a discount.

如果贵公司能大量订购我方产品，我方将给予折扣。

Buyers consider it too risky to buy large quantity at present because the market is uncertain.

买主认为目前大量购货太冒险，因为市场情况不定。

I can ask him if he can give us a better price if we buy in quantity.

如果我们要大量购买的话，我可以问他能否给我们比较优惠的价格。

7. profitable

profitable firm 盈利企业

They shared out a profitable domestic market and gave up competing on price.

它们共享一个利润丰厚的国内市场，并没有价格竞争。

A firm will enter the industry if such an action would be profitable.

如果一种行动有利可图，就会有企业进入这市场。

8. potential

market potential 市场潜力；市场潜在需求量

development potential 发展潜力；发展前景

potential market 潜在市场

Refrigeration industry in China has a long-term development potential.

中国制冷行业具有长期发展潜力。

In China, we must now consider how to deal with the huge potential market.

在中国，我们现在应考虑如何面对这个巨大的潜在市场。

Women make up half the potential market for most new electronic products.

女性用户占多数新型电子产品潜在市场份额的一半。

9. **CC : Carbon copy** 抄送

BCC : blind carbon copy 密送

 Expressions

○ For greetings

I'm very glad to receive your e-mail dated...

I thank you for your e-mail of...

○ For requests

I would appreciate/be grateful if you could ...

Could you please provide...? (more information)

I am writing to inform/apply for request...

○ For more information/feedbacks/suggestions

Thank you and look forward to having your opinion on...

Look forward to your feedbacks and suggestions soon.

What is your opinion on...

Further to our telephone conversation...

Part III
Practical Writing

Sample Consolidation

♣ Practice 1

Complete the information according to the samples.

	Sample 1	Sample 2
Subject of E-mail:		
Receiver:		
Intention:		
Requirements:		

Grammar Focus

The Passive Voice

◆ The basic form of passive voice:

be + (not) + p.p.

e.g.: Carriage is not covered by quotation.

How could she be persuaded to accept your offer?

◆ The situations where passive voice is used:

Generally speaking, English passive voice is preferable in the following situations.

1. When the action subject is unknown or cannot be readily stated.

   e.g.: This pro-forma invoice is supplied for applying for the necessary import license.

2. When the actor (doer of the action) is known but unnecessary to be mentioned.

   e.g.: Visitors are requested not to touch the exhibits.

3. When the actor is emphasized for some special purpose.

   e.g.: The three stores can be managed by a single experienced manager.

4. When the passive structure is used as a stylistic device to avoid the incoherence of structure shifting:

   e.g.: John was the representative of the company and was entrusted to deal with labor dispute.

◆ The main tenses of the passive voice:

Tense	Voice	Subject	Verb	Object
Simple Present	Active	Rita	sends	an e-mail.
	Passive	An e-mail	is sent	by Rita.
Simple Past	Active	Rita	sent	an e-mail.
	Passive	An e-mail	was sent	by Rita.
Present Perfect	Active	Rita	has sent	an e-mail.
	Passive	An e-mail	has been sent	by Rita.
Simple Future	Active	Rita	will send	an e-mail.
	Passive	An e-mail	will be sent	by Rita.
Past Perfect	Active	Rita	had sent	an e-mail.
	Passive	An e-mail	had been sent	by Rita.
Present Progressive	Active	Rita	is sending	an e-mail.
	Passive	An e-mail	is being sent	by Rita.

♣ Practice 2

Complete the following sentences with the correct form of the words in the parentheses.

1. —How long _____ you (employ) at this job?

   —Since 1990.

2. —What happened to the ordered goods from your company?

   —They _____ (destroy) in the earthquake.

3. Our catalogue _____ (send) to you for your reference next week.

4. No settlement _____ (reach) after the negotiation.

5. I don't know what decisions _____ (make) at the product development conference as John hasn't reported to me yet.

6. All the preparations for the new product _____ (complete), and we're ready to bring it into operation.

7. Hundreds of jobs _____ (lose) if the factory closes.

8. A new manufacturing shop _____ (build) here. They hope to finish it next month.

9. After the professional training, the staff went out of the meeting room one by one, only Mary _____ (leave).

10. The boss told the division managers that they _____ (expect) to be perfect in the performance evaluation (业绩评估).

♣ Practice 3

Change the following sentences into passive voice.

1. We have been talking about the issue of the reform of the management mode for years.

2. The personnel supervisor will ask every applicant a question about business.

3. We cannot accept your previous quotation.

4. Members of the board of directors will have to adopt a different attitude.

5. Your company should lay special emphasis on choice of payment.

6. We know that the cargo ship reached the South Pole in May.

Language Points

♣ Practice 4

Match each word to the correct definition.

1. enquire	a. the possibility of future success
2. quality	b. to impart knowledge of some fact, state or affairs, or event to
3. prospect	c. to conduct an inquiry or investigation of
4. inform	d. a distinct part that can be specified separately in a group of things that could be enumerated on a list
5. item	e. an essential and distinguishing attribute of something or someone
6. arrange	f. to put into a proper or systematic order; make arrangements for

1. _____ 2. _____ 3. _____ 4. _____ 5. _____ 6. _____

♣ Practice 5

Complete the following sentences with the proper form of the words in the box.

quantity	forecast	enquire	arrange	prospect	profit

1. Could you _____ a talk to a taxman for me?
2. To _____ about our Internet service plan details and other value-added service.
3. The twisted road leads to a bright _____.
4. I believe we can satisfy your requirement for any reasonable _____.
5. Airlines were _____ in 2007, but otherwise have been in loss every year since 2010.
6. Last, put forward to _____ the three greatest trends of Chinese search engine.

♣ Practice 6

Complete the following sentences in English.

1. _____ (你们对上述问题回复后), we will decide which option we would like to pursue.
2. Our company will be very happy _____ (在任何时候收到贵方订单).
3. Please check _____ (有关今天会议记录的附件).
4. _____ (期待您的反馈) and suggestions soon.
5. At your convenience, I would really appreciate your _____ (调查这件事情).
6. I sincerely _____ (为误解道歉).

Letter Practice

TEMPLATE

Heading
    To: _____
    From: _____
    Date:
    Subject:

Body:
    purpose; request; introduction; expectation; desire...

Signature

♣ Practice 7

Compose an e-mail letter with the given information according to the template above.

A. we are sending you by air a catalogue together with a range of pamphlets for reference

B. we require the name of your bank for credit investigation

C. listed in the catalogue

D. you wish to enter into business relationship with our corporation

E. Our quotation will be forwarded without any delay

To: Helen99@baibu.com.hk
From: shikil@siufit.com.
Date: 9 November 2011
Subject: business cooperation

Dear Mr. Green,

In reference to your letter of November 6th, 2011, we are glad to know that (1) _____ in the line of paper. In compliance with your request, (2) _____. If any of the items (3) _____ meets your interest, please let us have your special inquiry. (4) _____.

Prior to the conclusion of the first transaction between us, (5) _____.

Yours sincerely,
Tom Kerry
Manager of Export Department

🍀 Practice 8

Complete the e-mail below in English according to the Chinese in the parentheses.

Dear Mr. Zhang,

We are happy to report good sales of the new Language Translator (Model ZS 408). Our customers think that (1) _____ (这种袖珍机型在翻译单词和短语时非常有用).
Because the machines are most popular of all among business people, and (2) _____ (我们写信告知贵方) of numerous requests which they have made for the translators to include a number of common business terms.

(3) _____ (一些从事外贸的顾客也在咨询) if it is possible for Japanese, Arabic and Indonesian to be added to the 4 languages in the translator.

Unfortunately, however, (4) _____ (翻译机放到衣袋里太大太重) and too small to put in a briefcase. A small leather case is now urgently required for the machines.

Finally, we are happy to inform you that (5) _____ (电子词典销售得很好), and I now wish to order a further 200 electric dictionaries in addition to the 300 language translators previously ordered.

I look forward to hearing from you.

Yours sincerely,
Yao Lu
Sales Manager

♣ Practice 9

Write a reply to the above e-mail according to the information below.

Special cards should be produced, which can be fitted into the translators to provide more languages in the next model. Because the casing used now is very strong and furthermore, a leather case will make the price of our machines rise, the inclusion of leather case might not be necessary. Two hundred electronic dictionaries and three hundred language translators will be sent by the end of this week.

Part Ⅳ Supplementary Reading

Reading One

From: beth987@bbt.com.cn
To: yugkgd@jugy.com
Date: 22 May, 2011
Subject: Unable to accept special order

Dear Mr Wang,

We were pleased to receive your letter of May 20 concerning your special request.

We always take special orders, changing colors or materials for each particular order. However, we must take into consideration many factors carefully before we can accept the order.

I have spoken to the production manager in charge of costing. I am sorry to report that even if we did the job for you at cost, it would come out well above the price you are willing to pay.

I am checking with other manufacturers in this area who are dealing with the materials you want. They may be able to offer you the quality you want at a fair price. I will contact you once we get any information.

We appreciate your business and are so pleased that you inquired about this job. When you have a special need next time, please tell us again. We will try our best to meet your needs. If we cannot, we will try to find a company that can.

Yours sincerely,
Lu Guan
Lu Guan

To: jskayu@gsy.com
From: nxsai@dsu.com
Cc: hjk@huji.com
Subject: reply to your enquiry

Dear Mr. Zhao,

I have to acknowledge with thanks the receipt of your favor of June 15. We are so pleased to hear that you are interested in our products.

As you request, we are sending you a copy of our latest catalogues, together with some material samples we regularly use in our products, but I regret to say that we cannot send you the full range of samples as you requested. However, we can offer you other materials, such as leather and alloy material, which are of the same high quality.

Mrs. Green, our South Asian Sales Manager, will be in the Maldives next week and will be pleased to show you a wide range of our products. We think that you will agree that the best quality materials and the high standard of workmanship will appeal to buyers when you see them.

We also manufacture a wide range of leather and metal handicrafts which you may be interested in. They are fully illustrated in our catalogue and are of the same high quality as our handbags. Mrs. Green will be able to show you samples.

Should you be interested in any of our products, please let us know. We are willing to enter into business with your firm on the basis of equality, mutual benefit and exchanging what one has for what one needs.

Your favorable information will be appreciated.

Yours sincerely,
Helen

Memos

Objectives

To be proficient in

◎ understanding useful words and expressions often used in memos

◎ writing memos

◎ dealing with dangling modifiers correctly

Cultural Tips

Memorandum, memo for short, is commonly used to elaborate on a specific problem and an argument based on it for the convenience of reference. A memo usually includes the following contents: receiver, sender, date, subject, body. It tends to end with a brief and clear statement of what the action is as a reminder.

Part I
Warm-up Activities

◆ **Work in pairs and write down the key elements included in a memo.**

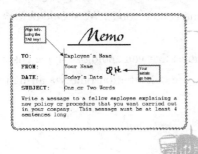

◆ **Fill in the blanks in the memo below according to the information in the card.**

> The general manager, Ron Wyden, decides to hold a meeting regarding quality control. The meeting will be held in Room 217 at 3p.m. on November 20th. He would like all department managers to attend the meeting. He wishes to write a business memo on November 18th in order to inform them of it.

MEMORANDUM

TO: _____

FROM: _____

DATE: _____

SUBJECT: _____

MESSAGE:

A meeting on quality control will be held in _____ at 3 p.m. on November 20th.

Ron Wyden

Part II
Sample Study

○ Sample 1

MEMORANDUM

TO: Peter Wang, *Distribution* Centre Director

FROM: Ralph Chen, General Manager

DATE: May 21st, 2011

SUBJECT: Handling a *Complaint* Letter

This memo relates to the handling of the complaint received on May 20th regarding a delivery error in order No. 622.

After verifying the causes, we believe it is our fault. We have already apologized to the customer on behalf of the company and promised to exchange the goods. We should *deliver* the correct goods in 3 days.

In order to *maintain* the company's *reputation*, I request that you apologize to the customer yourself. Additionally, you should ensure that the goods are delivered on time via airmail and that the wrongly delivered goods are gotten back.

Ralph Chen

Sample 2

MEMORANDUM

TO: Mark Song, Marketing Manager

FROM: Tony Smith, HR Manager

DATE: Dec. 2nd, 2011

SUBJECT: Personnel Changes

This memo is to *inform* you of some recent personnel changes.

◇ Helen has been *transferred* from the Advertising Department to the Human Resources Department.

◇ There will be two employees going to your department to assist your work next Monday according to your *request*.

◇ A training course should be organized because there are so many new employees. It will start next Wednesday and run for 3 weeks. Please inform all relevant members.

Tony Smith

Vocabulary

distribution	/ˌdistri'bjuːʃən/	n. 分布，分发
deliver	/di'livə/	v. 递送，交付
maintain	/mein'tein/	v. 维持，维修
reputation	/ˌrepju'teiʃən/	n. 名声，声誉
inform	/in'fɔːm/	v. 通知，告诉
transfer	/træns'fəː/	n.&v. 转移；调任
request	/ri'kwest/	n.&v. 请求，要求

Notes

1. memo=memorandum 备忘录

   A word originating from Latin, is often used to inform and remind the recipient of certain action to be carried out by sending informal messages among employees within a company.

2. HR =Human Resources 人力资源

3. AD =advertisement 广告

4. Marketing Manager 市场经理

HR Manager 人事部经理

Distribution Centre Director 物流中心主任

General Manager 总经理

5. personnel changes 人事变动

Expressions

Please ensure...

In order to maintain...

This memo is to confirm...

Please inform...

Part III
Practical Writing

Sample Consolidation

♣ Practice 1

Complete the information according to the samples.

	Sample 1	**Sample 2**
Receiver:	_____	_____
Sender:	_____	_____
Date:	_____	_____
Subject:	_____	_____

Grammar Focus

A Dangling Modifier

A dangling modifier refers to any word or phrase in a sentence, which should be consistent with the main sentence, but there is no correct consistency between them. It generally appears at the beginning of the sentence as an adverbial modifier. A dangling modifier is a common error in writing a sentence. The error types and correction ways will be discussed as below:

Main Error Types:

◇ Participle modifier

e.g.: Performing well on the stock market, the company's reputation grew.

◇ Prep.+gerund modifier

e.g.: By organizing your time well, the work has been done efficiently.

◇ Infinitive phrase modifier

e.g.: To understand the market well, investors welcomed him.

◇ Elliptical clause modifier

e.g.: While buying the guitar, it needs tuning.

Correction Ways:

◇ To modify the dangling part, make it consistent with the main sentence. e.g.:

Using the data collected by the technical team, an effective promotional campaign was implemented. (×)

Because the sales team used the data collected by the technical team, an effective promotional campaign was implemented. (√)

◇ To modify the main sentence, make its subject consistent with the logical subject modified by the dangling part. e.g.:

After verifying the complaint, it is necessary to exchange the goods. (×)

After verifying the complaint, we should exchange the goods. (√)

♣ Practice 2

Write a "D" in the blanks for the sentences which include dangling modifiers and an "N" for the sentences which do not.

1. Owing to lack of funds, the project was shelved. (   )
2. To win the competition, the price is reduced. (   )
3. Judging from your expression, the negotiation must have been very difficult. (   )
4. Dining at our annual meeting, the formal dress is required. (   )
5. By providing a better work environment, work efficiency can be improved. (   )
6. Taking into consideration the attractive profits, the work is definitely worthwhile. (   )

♣ Practice 3

Correct the dangling errors in the following sentences.

1. To adapt to a new working environment, the training is needed.
2. To be a loyal employee, a sense of belonging is a must.
3. Opening the cases, the shipment is not in accordance with my orders.
4. Under-performing and overpriced, the company investors purchased the shares.
5. Walking or sleeping, this business contract is always on his mind.
6. Dealing with business, it is necessary to keep honest and effective communications between both parties.

Language Points

♣ Practice 4

Match each word to the correct definition.

1. complaint
2. deliver
3. verify
4. reputation

a. to state that something is truth; check
b. an expression of discontent
c. a worker who is hired to perform a job
d. to take goods to the place where they have been sent

5. inform   e. the state of being held in high esteem and honor

6. employee   f. to tell someone about something

1. _____   2. _____   3. _____   4. _____   5. _____   6. _____

♣ Practice 5

Complete the following sentences with the proper form of the words in the box.

complain	distribute	deliver	inform	employ	transfer

1. They could not agree on the _____ of the profits.

2. The _____ of money online is very common today.

3. Please _____ us of your current special offers.

4. Can you _____ the goods within 24 hours?

5. He was requested to report the _____ to the committee.

6. He was promoted from an _____ to an employer within a short time.

♣ Practice 6

Complete the following sentences in English.

1. I knew that _____ (商务会议推到周日了).

2. Did you _____ (看到备忘录) sent you yesterday ?

3. _____ (为了维护公司的声誉), we should strive to provide the best possible service to all of our customers.

4. In accordance with the company policy, all members of staff must ensure that _____ (货物能够及时空运过去).

5. _____ (考虑到如此多的新人), it is inevitable that we must invest more into training and development.

Letter Practice

TEMPLATE

MEMO

To: _____

From: _____

Date: _____

Subject: description of the _____ in the memo

Body:

Introduce the background of the memo briefly.

Describe the main point(s) of the memo.

Let the readers know what they should do after receiving the memo.

Complimentary Close:

Signature:

Practice 7

Compose a memo with the given information according to the template above.

A. Please provide us your view on

B. enforcing a smoking ban on company premises

C. I would like to receive your report

D. The effect it would have on staff morale

E. Whether we should implement this policy

MEMORANDUM

From: The Managing Director

To: The Personnel Manager, Division A

Date: 27th May, 2011

Subject: Enforcement of a Smoking Ban

The Board is thinking of (1) _____ . Before we take this action, we would appreciate if you could share your views on the following issues:

1. (2) _____ .

2. Any potential issue that might arise when implementing the ban.

(3) _____ :

◇ How the staff will react to the idea.

◇ Whether restricting employees from smoking on premises will improve productivity.

◇ (4) _____ .

If possible, (5) _____ before the next Board meeting on 1st June.

Dacio Anderson

Practice 8

Write a memo according to the information below.

Imagine you are Mr. Lee, the Managing Director. As the company's annual profit has doubled, you decide to distribute an iPhone 4S to every frontline salesperson in the Marketing Department as an extra reward to express your gratitude. The memo should be sent to Xiao Hua, the Sales Manager on 19th Feb., 2011.

Part IV
Supplementary Reading

Reading One

Grand China Holdings

MEMORANDUM

To: Lisa Smith, General Manager

From: Linda Yao, Office Assistant

Date: 12th Dec., 2011

Subject: Purchase of a Coffee Machine

1. Introduction

In accordance with the request which you made at the recent staff meeting on Wednesday, 7th Dec., 2011, I would now like to present details relating to the coffee machine purchase by the company.

2. Background

There are an increasing number of coffee-loving personnel in our company.

3. Advantage

Having our own coffee machine would mean that members of staff can return to work on time after lunch. There is no need to waste valuable time going out to purchase coffee.

4. Staff Opinion

A survey found that all staff would prefer to use the company's own coffee machine.

5. Requirement

A sum of $500 is required in order to purchase a coffee machine.

I would kindly appreciate it if you could approve this purchase.

Linda Yao

Reading Two

MEMO

To: James Liu, Sales Department Manager

From: Sam Yu, Salesperson

Date: 10 Jan., 2011

Subject: Notification of My Resignation

I am writing to inform you of my intention to resign from my current role with Pacific High Pty Ltd.

It has not been an easy decision for me at all, especially taking into consideration all the great support and training you have given me over the last 3 years which has allowed me to transform from a fresh graduate into a leading salesperson. However, I feel it is the right time for me to move on to challenge myself in a new environment.

In accordance with the company's resignation policy, I am now giving 4 weeks' notice to the company. I will leave the company on the 10th of February. In the mean time, I will ensure that all my current work is completed in a timely manner. I am more than willing to train a replacement if the company thinks it is necessary.

Once again, thank you for your continued support.

Lesson Thirteen · ● ●

Minutes

Objectives

To be proficient in

◎ understanding the useful words and expressions often used in minutes

◎ writing minutes

◎ using basic skills of shorthand

Cultural Tips

Minutes are a brief summary of proceedings at meetings. It usually includes the following contents: heading, attendees, non-attendants, special attendees, endorsement of last minutes, new business, place, time and date of the next meeting, signatures of Chairperson and Secretary.

Part I
Warm-up Activities

◆ **Work in pairs. Write out the key elements included in minutes.**

Minutes of the company monthly meeting
Nov. 11, 2011

Present: Sun Ting
Absent: Zhang Ling

1. Minutes of last meeting
   All the projects were finished as scheduled
2. New business
   ...
3. Adjournment
the meeting was adjourned at
12:00 am.

Signature

_____

_____

_____

_____

_____

◆ **Complete the brief minutes below according to the following picture.**

Title: The monthly meeting of _____

Date: _____

Location: Room 207

_____: Susan Wang, Brant Smith…

Summary of the meeting:

_____ who have had outstanding performance last year.

_____ in the new year.

Adjournment:

There being no other business to discuss, the meeting was adjourned at _____.

Part II
Sample Study

○ Sample 1

Minutes of the Company *Monthly* Meeting

Shenzhen Yantong Industry Group Co., Ltd.

November 20, 2011

Room 308

**Easy 4 me 2 Learn
Writing Meeting
Minutes and Agendas**
Lots of exercises and
free downloadable workbook
Heather Baker

Present: Sun Ting (Chair), Liu Xin, Li Bin,

Jiang Hua, Wang Fang (Secretary)

Absent: Apologies were received from Zhang Ling

1. Minutes of Last Meeting

H.R. Dept. Manager, Liu Xin, made a *motion* that the minutes of the meeting on October 25 had been *approved* and distributed.

2. Matters *Arising*

All the projects were finished on schedule.

3. New Business

◇ The Board of Directors moved that since the sales performance is very noticeable, all official staffs will get a salary increase of three percent.

◇ Production Dept. Manager *recommended* purchasing the advanced equipment and expanding production scale.

◇ Those who had shown outstanding performance or had put forward some useful suggestions to the company will be rewarded according to the convention.

4. Announcements

The next monthly meeting will be held on December 20, 2011, and the exact time and location will be announced in the meeting notice.

5. *Adjournment*

There was no other business to be discussed, and the meeting was adjourned at 12:00 a.m.

(signature)
Wang Fang (Secretary)

○ Sample 2

Minutes of the Company Board
February 22, 2011
Room 6115

Attendees: Doris Spears, Jon White Bear, Douglas Carver, Lee Miller, Pat Kyumoto, Jack Porter, Mary Rifkin and Leslie Zevon

Absent: Joan Barnes

1. Last Meeting Minutes

The minutes of last meenting was *amended* and approved.

2. Chief Executive's Report

The Chief Executive recommended that if we are not able to find a new facility by the end of this month, the organization should stay in the current location over the winter. After brief discussion, the Board agreed.

3. Finance Committee Report Provided by Chair, Lee Miller

Miller explained that the consultant, Susan Johns, reviewed the organization's bookkeeping procedures in preparation for the upcoming yearly financial audit and found them to be satisfactory.

4. Board Development Committee's Report Provided by Chair, Douglas Carver

Carver reminded the Board of the planned cancellation of the real estate project in three months and provided a drafted project cancellation schedule for board *review*.

5. Adjournment

The meeting was adjourned at 9:30 a.m.

Minutes *submitted* by Secretary, Doris Spears.

Vocabulary

minutes	/'minits/	n. 会议记录，备忘录
monthly	/'mʌnθli/	adj. 每月的
motion	/'məuʃən/	n. 示意，提议，动议
approve	/ə'pruːv/	v. 批准，赞成
arise	/ə'raiz/	v. 出现，升起，发生
recommend	/ˌrekə'mend/	v. 推荐，建议，劝告
adjournment	/ə'dʒəːnmənt/	n. 休会，休会期间
amend	/ə'mend/	v. 修正，改进
review	/ri'vjuː/	v. 检查；复审；回顾
submit	/səb'mit/	v. 提交，呈递

Notes

1. minutes of the company monthly meeting 公司月会纪要

   minutes 会议记录（只有复数形式）

2. new business 新议题

3. matters arising 续议事项，前议事项，上次会议记录所提事项

4. Production Dept. Manager 生产部经理

5. Chief Executive 行政总裁，首席执行官

6. Finance Committee 财务部

7. real estate project 房地产项目

Expressions

Apologies were received from...

All the projects were finished on schedule.

The board of directors moved/recommended that...

The next monthly meeting will be held at...

Meeting minutes were amended and approved.

Part III Practical Writing

Sample Consolidation

♣ Practice 1

Complete the information according to the samples.

	Sample 1	Sample 2
Date:		
Place:		
Present:		
Absent:		
Adjournment:		

Grammar Focus

Shorthand

Shorthand is a speed writing method that allows people to use special signs or shorter forms to represent letters, words or phrases. A typical shorthand method uses abbreviations for words and common phrases, which can allow someone well-trained in the system to write as quickly as people speak. The basic skill of shorthand is that vowels in the words need to be omitted.

e.g.: Do you need to write a message to him?

D u nd t wt a msg t hm?

♣ Practice 2

Give the words below in shorthand form.

1. we   2. he   3. you
4. told   5. message 6. be able to do

♣ Practice 3

Write longhand of the following.

1. th chm ajrd th mtn utl th fllw dy?

2. It is a gd opr.

3. Whi is h so lt?

4. t dlvr th gds asnsps

5. Th lwyr gv th grl sm gd advc.

6. Th mngr o th htl ws v k t thm.

♣ Practice 4

Match each word to the correct definition.

1. recommend	a. to give a plan, piece of writing etc. to someone in authority for them to consider or approve
2. adjournment	b. to happen
3. amend	c. to make amendments to; to make better
4. submit	d. to suggest that a particular action should be done
5. motion	e. suggestion at meeting
6. arise	f. having a pause or rest during a formal meeting or trial

1. _____ 2. _____ 3. _____ 4. _____ 5. _____ 6. _____

♣ Practice 5

Complete the following sentences with the proper form of the words in the box.

arise	motion	submit	adjourn	approve	recommend

1. Could I ask if you will _____ the project?

2. The meeting will be postponed or _____ to a future date.

3. If you were in urgent need of the goods, I'd like to _____ Article 58.

4. Serious obligations may _____ from the misunderstanding of the motion.

5. He _____ a market research report to his boss.

6. The board is now debating the _____ and will vote on it shortly.

♣ Practice 6

Complete the following sentences in English.

1. According to _____ (上月会议纪要), we will move to the new office building in June .

2. _____ (依据惯例), we need to send the top sales to attend the annual meeting in Los Angeles.

3. Last month our general manager was invited to _____ (就团队建设做了简短的演讲).

4. The exact location and time of the next monthly meeting will _____ (见会议通知).

5. Can we begin by _____ (讨论上次会议产生的问题)?

Letter Practice

TEMPLATE

Opening:

The meeting of the _____ was held in the place on date.

Present: _____

Absent: name list of persons not present

Minutes of Last Meeting:

Matters Arising:

New Business:

Summarize the discussion for new issues.

Announcements:

The next meeting will be held at time on date in location.

Adjournment:

The meeting was _____ at time by…

Minutes Submitted by:

Signature:

♣ Practice 7

Compose the minutes with the given information according to the template above.

A. the minutes of the meeting on May 15 had been approved

B. the exact location will be given by e-mail

C. Apologies were received from Eve Gu

D. the meeting was adjourned at 12:00 a.m.

E. show new products and expand production scale

Minutes of the Company Weekly Meeting

Beijing IBM AD Group Co., Ltd.

May 20, 2011

Room 220

Present: Mary Wang (Chair), Peter Liu, Judy Chen, Herry Hao (Secretary)

Absent: (1) _____.

1. Minutes of Last Meeting

Sales Manager Jason Jiang made a motion that (2) _____.

2. Matters Arising

All the projects were finished as scheduled.

3. New Business

New employees should improve their communication ability with customers because of the complaints received by the General Manager.

A.D. Manager recommended that a famous model should be invited to (3) _____

_____.

4. Announcements

The next meeting will be held at 10:00 a.m. on Monday, May 27, 2011, and (4) _____

_____.

5. Adjournment

There being no other business to be discussed, (5) _____.

Respectfully submitted.

(signature)

Wang Fang, Secretary

May 20, 2011

A.D.=advertisement

♣ Practice 8

Complete the minutes according to the Chinese in the parentheses.

(1) _____ (年度会议纪要)

The Grand China Express

Dec. 23, 2011

Chairing: Mr. Li Zhe

Present: Mr. Wang Dong, Mr. Zhao Lei, Ms. Zhou Yan

RM: 105

Absent: Ms. Jane Chen

Successfully organized the summer camp for China B&B Company.

(2) _____ (销售额达到5百万元，收益30万元).

(3) _____ (下次会议地点不变) on Feb. 22, 2012.

(4) _____ (会议下午5点结束).

Submitted by Mr. Li Zhe

Part IV
Supplementary Reading

Reading One

MINUTES

The Seminar on Cooperation Between A&B Company and U.S. Enterprises

February 12, 2011

9:30 a.m. —3:00 p.m.

Room 115 in the International Hotel

Present: Mr. Lee,　Mr. Zhou Baohua,　Ms. Xiao Zhang,

　　　　　Mr. Li Zhichao.　Ms. Janet,　Mr. James Eurbank,

　　　　　Ms. Maggie,　Mr. Li (Secretary)

Absent: No

1. Welcome and Call to Order—Mr. Lee

Mr. Lee welcomed all present members from A&B Company and U.S. enterprises and called the seminar to order at 9:30 a.m.

2. Discussion

Discussion on ways to expand the cooperation between A&B Company and U.S. enterprises—Representatives of the companies.

(1) To expand bilateral trade

On one hand, A&B Company, in accordance with domestic demand, has imported more agricultural and industrial products from the U.S. enterprises. On the other hand, U.S. enterprises should export more competitive products to A&B Company. In addition, the two sides should expand cooperation in service trade.

(2) To expand two-way investments

The companies on both sides should strive to create a fair and sound investment in products of the other side to enter their market.

(3) To explore new cooperation fields

Enterprises of the two sides should explore the feasibility of cooperation in the fields of clean energy, IT, new materials, and service sector.

3. Other

There were no other items.

4. Adjournment

Mr. Lee thanked everyone for their time. The seminar was adjourned at 3:00 p.m. The next seminar between A&B Company and U.S enterprises is scheduled on Feb. 21, 2012 in Grand China Hotel, Beijing.

Respectfully submitted

(signature)

Reading Two

Minutes of the Company Annual Meeting

Huayuan Trading Co., Ltd.

December 15, 2011

Room 1202, Beijing Kunlun International Hotel

Present: CHAN TAT, WAH SIMON,　CHEUNG TAI ON,　CHOW CHI WAI,

　　　DING KIN FUNG,　KWOK SHIU YEE,　CHUEN YUE

Absent: No

1. Minutes of Last Year's Meeting

The minutes had already been signed.

2. Matters Arising

All the projects were finished as scheduled.

3. Annual Report

(1) Exports amounted to US$ 122.2 million, a 16 percent growth year-on-year.

Exports of mechanic and electronic products, hi-tech products and processing products all surpassed 30 million US dollars in the year of 2011, setting a record high. Among those, exports of mechanic and electronic products reached US$ 20 million, accounting for 26% of foreign trade exports, and have maintained the status of the largest category of exported commodities for 5 consecutive years.

(2) Investment of US$ 6.6 million achieved in China.

(3) The building of a new enterprise promoted during the 2nd Five-year Plan period.

4. Announcements

The next meeting will be held on December 27, 2012 and the exact location will be announced in the meeting notice.

5. Adjournment

The meeting was adjourned at 5:00 p.m.

Respectfully submitted.

(signature)

Business Reports

Objectives

To be proficient in
◎ understanding the useful words and expressions often used in business reports
◎ writing a business report
◎ using approximations

Cultural Tips

A report plays a crucial role in business practice, as most major or decisive actions are based on business reports. The purpose of a commercial report is to inform one or more persons about a special subject with facts and arguments. The basic parts of a business report include: introduction, findings, conclusions and recommendations.

Part I
Warm-up Activities

◆ **Work in pairs and choose the correct answers to the following question.**

What parts are involved in a business report?

Introduction: read the topic, _____;
Resources: _____, construct the report, graphic elements, cite the information;
Conclusion: _____, module summary.

A. produce report   B. redefine the scope   C. research sources

◆ **Brainstorm and discuss the steps of writing a business report.**

_____ the problem

_____ the reader

_____ the information

_____ the information

_____ the outline

_____ a draft

_____ the draft

Steps

Part II
Sample Study

Sample 1

On the Market Responses of the Newly-launched Toys

Introduction

This paper is formed to get to know the market responses of our newly-launched toys for young teenagers. 2,000 *questionnaires* were issued, of which 1,897 were returned. The summarizing report is as below, showing the positive and negative responses.

Findings

Responses of Questionnaires

a. levels of satisfactions

Overall 94.8% of customers *responded* to the investigations and 80% are interested in the new products. 16% are not attracted by the new one and the rest have a negative attitude to the launch.

b. points to attract teenagers

◇ Easy handling *via* automatic remote control

◇ *Motivation* to improve teenagers' intelligence

◇ Good to the environment

◇ Dedicate to the design with popular superstar *logo*

c. *deficiency*

Parents and teenagers are not so willing to accept the new concept of Green Products.

Conclusions

The vast majority of customers were interested in the newly-launched product. Although there is some negative feedbacks from the investigation, market response shows positive feedback. However, some points still need to be improved.

Recommendations

◇ Maintain and strengthen the *propagation* of Green knowledge as the new generated concept.

◇ Road-shows are needed to give the public a better understanding of the new products.

◇ We have to *gurantee* the relevant after-sales service level as doubts about new products occupied in the potential customers' mind.

Sample 2

On the Profit Status over Last Fiscal Years

Introduction

This report sets out to show the company's profit status to all employees and *shareholders*.

Overview

Sales amounts over last fiscal year achieved 44 million CHF, around 10% over the forecasted amounts. In region, European markets keep the same level as last year and Asia & Pacific markets show a strong motivation, with sales increased 20% compared with last year. However, the US markets are negative with sharp 30% decrease in sales. While the China domestic market shows a small increase which is anyway very good under such a terrible economic background.

Prosperity

The coming year is still not optimistic because of the bad global economic situation. However, we have strong confidence in the sales of next year when the increased sales percentage lies in the newly-launched project of "speed fish" catering to the middle rich level group.

Conclusions

◇ Profit status shows a very good end to the last fiscal year. Those who hold stocks will see profit of 3% for every share.

◇ We are very optimistic with the next year's sales and great confidence has been extended to the employees and stockholders.

◇ We will launch new projects to ensure that the aim of sales increase will be achieved.

Recommendations

Internal and external training needs to be strengthened to guarantee the qualification of sales people. Moreover, investment on product propagation and new sales staff *recruitment* need to be done to create a strong sales and service team for the new project.

Vocabulary

questionnaire	/ˌkwestʃə'nɛə/	*n.* 问卷，调查表
respond	/ri'spɔnd/	*v.* 应答
via	/'vaiə/	*prep.* 通过，经由，取道
motivation	/ˌməuti'veiʃən/	*n.* 动机，积极性，推动
logo	/'ləugəu/	*n.* 商标，徽标，标识语
deficiency	/di'fiʃənsi/	*n.* 缺乏，不足
propagation	/ˌprɔpə'geiʃən/	*n.* 宣传，传播
guarantee	/ˌgærən'tiː/	*v.* 保证；担保
shareholder	/'ʃɛəhəuldə/	*n.* 股东，股票持有人
recruitment	/ri'kruːtmənt/	*n.* 招聘

Notes

the newly-launched toy 新推出的玩具

profit status 利润状况

fiscal year 财务年度

CHF (Confederation Helvetica France) 瑞士法郎

Expressions

For Introduction

The purpose/aim of this report is…

The report aims to…

The report is based on…

For Findings

The key findings are outlined below.

It was found that…

The following points summarize our key findings.

For Conclusion

It is clear that…

No conclusions were reached regarding…

It was accepted/agreed that…

○ For Recommendations

It would be advisable to…

It is essential to…

We strongly recommend that…

Part III
Practical Writing

Sample Consolidation

♣ Practice 1

Read the samples again and choose the proper options to complete the table.

a. to show the profit status of the company

b. The profit status of the company saw a good end last fiscal year.

c. The majority of customers were interested in the newly launched product.

d. 80% of respondents were interested in the new products, but parents and teenagers are not so willing to accept the new concept of green product.

e. Sales amounts over last fiscal year achieved 44 million CHF.

f. Internal and external training needs to be strengthened.

g. Strengthen the green knowledge propagation

h. to know the market response of the newly-launched toy

	Sample 1	Sample 2
Purpose:	_____	_____
Findings:	_____	_____
Conclusions:	_____	_____
Recommendations:	_____	_____

Grammar Focus

Approximations

An approximation is the number, calculation or position that is close to a correct number, calculation or position, but is not exact. In report writing, we could use approximations to describe the section of findings, conclusions and recommendations.

Notes:

◇ Don't use fractions but use percentage where the denominator is greater than five.

e.g.: 37.5% of customers are very satisfied with our service.

◇ Don't forget the hyphen in fractions.

e.g.: Two-thirds of merchandise has been sold out.

◇ Don't use "a" or "one" in front of "half".

    e.g.: Half of the products were damaged in delivery.

◇ "Only" and "just" often refer to a negative meaning.

    e.g.: Only 1% of the candidates got ideal jobs.

♣ Practice 2

Choose the best answer to complete the sentences below.

1. _____ (Three-fourth/Three-fourths) of the surface in the world is made up of water.
2. Four-fifths of the goods _____ (was/were) delivered to the customers on time.
3. _____ (Only/About) 1% of the visitors to Greece were satisfied with their tourist guide.
4. _____ (One-quarter/A quarter) of the workers completed the task.
5. Two-thirds of _____ (employee/employees) in the company are less than 30 years old.
6. China is a huge country with a population of 1.3 billion. That is _____ (one-fifth/ one fifth) of the world's population.

♣ Practice 3

Correct the errors in the following sentences often used in business reports.

1. The population of our company is just 1, 511.
2. Five-seventh of the crew were rescued.
3. One half of the passengers were satisfied with their service.
4. Three quarter of the questionnaires were returned.
5. 50% of the employees' salary in my company has been raised this year.
6. 201 customers replied to the questionnaires.

Language Points

♣ Practice 4

Match each word to the correct definition.

1. CHF	a. a person who answers a request for information
2. guarantee	b. to be circulated or published
3. questionnaire	c. Confederation Helvetica France
4. logo	d. believing that good things will happen in the future
5. optimistic	e. the process of finding people to work for a company or become member of an organization
6. recruitment	f. a design or symbol used by a company to advertise its products
7. respondent	g. to make certain
8. issue	h. a list of questions that several people are asked so that information can be collected about something

1. _____ 2. _____ 3. _____ 4. _____ 5. _____ 6. _____ 7. _____ 8. _____

Practice 5

Complete the following sentences with the proper form of the words in the box.

response	satisfy	laptop	vary	suitable	promise

1. The Russian market is _____ because of the relatively stable political and economic situations there.

2. The purpose of this report is to assess the _____ of my position as Sales Manager for home-based working.

3. My working pattern and that of my colleagues _____ from week to week.

4. In America, to our great surprise, the sales of _____ was declining to some extent.

5. We should maintain the current high levels of _____ and use future questionnaires to monitor our performance.

6. Overall 94.8% of customers _____ to the investigation.

Practice 6

Translate the following sentences into English.
1. 如果您需要更多信息，请随时联系我们。
2. 兹介绍长虹公司，中国数一数二的电视机出口商。
3. 我想为朋友预订一晚的双人间一间。
4. 我们的产品远销英国、美国、日本和东南亚。
5. 我很遗憾地通知您，我们不能接受您的退款要求。
6. 我公司服装部拟聘一位全职销售员。

Report Practice

TEMPLATE

Introduction: consist of purpose, background, methodology, scope, etc.

Findings: present the selected _____ you have collected and analyzed systematically.

◇ make clear the topic;

◇ present _____ to convince;

◇ summarize and present the _____ in positive tone.

Conclusions: sum up the main _____ and make a logical deduction.

Recommendations: put forward practical _____ based on your findings and conclusions.

🍀 Practice 7

Compose a business report with the given information according to the template above.

A. Problems and its solutions

B. the course should focus on our students

C. The current situation of the school should be emphasized

D. We strongly recommend

E. The aim of this report is to recommend a one-day training session

---

Report on Recommendation for a One-day Training Session

Introduction

(1) _____ , called " Familiarity with Your Position", for our school counselors.

(2) _____:

We have employed 15 school counselors this term. Although they have work experience, they are not familiar with the new environment. So, a one-day training session is urgently needed.

Contents

Some brief information of the school should be given. (3) _____. These would probably create an affection with the school. Then, (4) _____. High enthusiasm should be put on the types, characteristics and needs of our students, which will help them feel more responsible for their work.

Recommendations

(5) _____ that training be arranged as soon as possible. It could be held on weekends.

🍀 Practice 8

Read the information below and complete the business report, adding details where necessary.

A shipping accident took place in the West Coast of Yangtze River on May 9, 2011. Due to the thick fog, two ships collided not far from Wuhan. It's lucky there were no casualties among the crews and passengers. A committee of the port authorities would be set up to investigate the cause.

You are secretary of the Customs Department and are required to write a research report about it. Your report should include the process, the cause, the results of the accident and the response of the authorities.

An Investigation Report on a Shipping Accident

To: The Custom Department Committee

From: John Jones, Secretary of the Customs Department

Date : May 10, 2011

Introduction:

(1) _____ a shipping accident off West Coast of the Yangtze River.

Investigations:

(2) _____. One was a cargo ship carrying lumber, apparently on its way to Changjiang. The other was a National ferry on a regular run from Jiujiang to Wuhan.

(3) _____, the captains did not realize the danger until a few seconds before the collision took place. Consequently, there was no time for them to prevent the accident.

(4) _____, but both ships suffered heavy damage.

Recommendations:

It is suggested that (5) _____.

🌸 Practice 9

Read and complete the following report according to the Chinese given in the parentheses.

To: Mr. Smith, General Manager

From: Tom Walker

Date: January 10, 2011

Subject: New Practices of JINXIANG Chain Fast Food Restaurants

Introduction

(1) _____ (总经理安排我写一份报告) on new experiences of staff management policies of the JINXIANG chain fast food restaurants, and (2) _____ (对公司的效益作出分析).

Findings

It was found that one of the JINXIANG restaurants is exposed to an exceptionally innovative management in order to maintain high-standard services to its guests. The two new practices are as follows:

(3) _____ (所有服务生) are exposed to a check-up before starting their lunch and dinner shifts so as to ensure maintenance of hygiene (卫生) and compliance with the company's dress code.

The evening briefings conducted on a regular basis which resulted in changes in the menu have proved effective.

Conclusions

(4) _____ (很显然) a successful introduction of the two procedures is sure to reflect on the waiting staff's better awareness of good services and will improve the company's image.

Recommendations

(5) _____ (我们极力建议) that these two procedures (staff's check-up and regular evening briefings) should be applied in the restaurant department of our company.

Part Ⅳ Supplementary Reading

Reading One

To: Black Hughes, Board Chairman

From: Evan Green

Date: Oct. 20, 2011

Subject: Assessment of Suitability for Home-based Working

This report sets out to access the suitability (适宜性) of my position as Market Innovation Specialist (市场创新专员) for home-based working.

There are some differences between my working pattern and that of my colleagues. A large part of my time is spent to do fieldwork, including visiting various advertising companies and browsing the Internet for the latest popular trends. Also, it is accompanied with various road shows and activities with distribution for product demonstration and advertising launches. The communication with colleagues varies from time to time or from place to place. But the same results can be achieved.

It is clear that I am able to undertake the duties while working from home for a large proportion of my time.

I would suggest that I should be given the necessary equipment to work from home.

Reading Two

To: Related Investors

From: Maria Li, Stock Broker

Date: May 15, 2011

Subject: Investment in the Pacific Cosmetics Company

Introduction

The purpose of this report is to provide you with financial data necessary to make your investment decisions on the Pacific Cosmetics Company.

The Pacific Cosmetics Company, a multinational company (跨国公司) and a national leader in cosmetics business, has been developing new kinds of products to meet different people's needs and personal preferences (个人爱好) of consumers.

Findings

The Pacific Cosmetics Company owns 45% of the cosmetics market. It is attempting to expand its market share by using advertising campaigns. The company is undertaking health care (保健养生) business.

In 2010, sales went up by 18% compared with the previous year. This is the fifteenth consecutive year that sales have increased. Earning (利润) rose by 14% compared with the previous year.

Conclusions

The company's financial position (财务状况) is clearly very strong. It shows a steady growth in both sales and profits.

Recommendations

I think that buying the Pacific Cosmetics Company's stock would be a very wise investment.

Commercial Advertising

Objectives

To be proficient in

◎ understanding the useful words and expressions often used in commercial advertising

◎ writing a commercial advertisement

◎ using rhetorical devices in advertisements

Cultural Tips

In our daily life, advertisements often refer to commercial advertisements, which are a paid-form of presentation or promotion of goods and services. Advertising's role is to create a positive image of a product or service. An advertisement usually consists of three parts: headline, body and slogan.

Part I
Warm-up Activities

◆ **Work in pairs and write out the Chinese brand name of the following advertisements.**

_____   _____   _____

◆ **Write out the slogans of the above product advertisements in English.**

车到山前必有路, 有路必有丰田车。(丰田汽车)

非常可乐，非常选择。(可口可乐)

同一个世界，同一个梦想。(2008年奥运会)

成功之路，从头开始。(飘柔洗发水)

我就喜欢。(麦当劳)

味道好极了。(雀巢咖啡)

Part II
Sample Study

○ **Sample 1**

To Rent

Location: JIN BI APARTMENT is located at No. 480, Yuhua District, Changsha

Description:

◇ unfurnished, new paint, *laundry facilities*;

◇ gas, water, power, and parking available;

◇ 1-bedroom, 2-bedroom and 3-bedroom apartments for rent or co-rent, *condos* for rent, and *townhouses* for rent;

◇ price ranges from RMB 400 to RMB 2,000 per month.

For availability and more details about *rental*, please call us TOLL FREE 400-400-4000

Contact: Chen Xiang, Rental Office

Phone: 0731-88888888

○ **Sample 2**

Aokang Leather Shoes

Aokang Shoes Co. Ltd. is one of the top 100 private *enterprises* in China, which specializes in producing and selling leather shoes.

Aokang leather shoes sell well not only in the mainland of China, but also in places as far as Italy, Spain, America, and Japan. With excellent designs, *fashionable* styles, fine *workmanship*, and rich varieties, Aokang leather shoes are highly praised and *appreciated* by the consuming public. In terms of annual turnover, the company has been among the best in China.

Services offered: a one-year *warranty*

one-month change guarantee

Wear Aokang, go everywhere!

Manufacturer: Aokang Shoes Co. Ltd.

Tel.: 0577-67288888

Website: http://www.aokang.com

Vocabulary

laundry	/'lɔːndri/	n. 洗衣店，洗衣房
facility	/fə'siliti/	n. 设施，设备
condo	/'kɔndəu/	n. 公寓套房
townhouse	/'taunhaus/	n. 城市屋，小楼房
rental	/'rentəl/	n. 租赁
enterprise	/'entəpraiz/	n. 企业
fashionable	/'fæʃənəbl/	adj. 流行的，时髦的
workmanship	/'wəːkmənʃip/	n. 手艺，工艺，技巧
appreciate	/ə'priːʃieit/	v. 欣赏，感激
warranty	/'wɔrənti/	n. 保证，担保

Notes

laundry facility	洗衣设施
toll free	免费电话
private enterprise	民营企业

Expressions

Gas, water and power available…

We provide the following services:

For more details, please contact…

New varieties are introduced one after another.

Fashionable styles, rich varieties.

Excellent quality, a good reputation over the world, orders are welcome.

Part III
Practical Writing

Sample Consolidation

♣ Practice 1

Complete the information according to the samples.

Sample 1

Room Types: _____

Price: _____

Contact Information: _____

Sample 2

Headline: _____

Slogan: _____

Name of company: _____

Grammar Focus
Rhetorical Devices in Advertisement

Rhetoric plays a very important role in English advertisements and acts as a key element for the success of an advertisement. It includes similes, metaphors, puns, personifications, parallelisms, and repetitions. e.g.:

Light as a breeze, soft as a cloud. (simile)

Breakfast without orange juice like a day without sunshine. (simile)

You're better off under the Umbrella. (metaphor)

The Unique Spirit of Canada. (pun)

Unlike me, my Rolex never needs a rest. (personification)

It provides you with beauty. It provides you with joy. It provides you with love. It provides you with fun. (parallelism)

Finish the job in less time, with less fuel and less noise. (repetition)

Practice 2

Choose the best answer to the rhetorical features of the following ads.

1. Apple thinks different. (personification / simile)
2. Today, it is like a thriving sakura. (metaphor / simile)
3. Ask for More. (pun / repetition)
4. The world smiles with *Reader's Digest*. (pun / personification)
5. Take TOSHIBA, take the world. (parallelism / pun)
6. We don't just want you to clean your teeth. We want to help you keep them. (personification/ parallelism)
7. As soft as Mother's hands. (simile / metaphor)
8. Extraordinary Cola, Extraordinary Choice. (repetition / parallelism)
9. Henan in China—the cradle of China martial arts. (simile / metaphor)
10. Make up your mind before you make up your face. (repetition / personification)

Practice 3

Match the following English slogans to the Chinese ones and then point out their rhetorical features.

(   ) 1. Better late than the late.
(   ) 2. Featherwater. Light as a feather.
(   ) 3. She works while you rest.
(   ) 4. No business too small, no problem too big.
(   ) 5. Kodak is Olympic color.
(   ) 6. Mosquito bye bye bye.

A. 没有做不了的小生意，没有解决不了的大问题。

B. 她工作，你休息。

C. Featherwater眼镜：轻如鸿毛。

D. 蚊子杀、杀、杀。

E. 宁停三分，不抢一秒。

F. 柯达就是奥林匹克的色彩。

Language Points

Practice 4

Match each word to the correct definition.

1. enterprise   a. to use fuel, energy or time, esp. in large amounts
2. townhouse   b. authority; (written or printed) guarantee
3. apartment   c. company, business
4. facilities   d. a house that is joined to another house

5. warranty   e. a set of rooms for living in, especially on one floor of a building

6. consume   f. equipment and services provided for a particular purpose

1. _____   2. _____   3. _____   4. _____   5. _____   6. _____

❖ Practice 5

Complete the following sentences with the proper form of the words in the box.

desire	hospitable	confirm	according	cooperate	refund

1. The above offer (报价) is subject to our final _____. We advise you to place a quick order.

2. Please supply the goods in strict _____ with the details as follows.

3. This is to thank you for your _____ on this matter.

4. We are able to _____ your money without shipping cost.

5. I am writing this letter to thank you for your warm _____ accorded to me and my delegation during our recent visit to your beautiful country.

6. On my graduation from college this fall, I am _____ to secure a position that will offer me opportunities in the field of import and export trading.

❖ Practice 6

Complete the following sentences in English.

1. I _____ (毫不犹豫地) in recommending the position for you.

2. _____ (非常感谢您能邀请我), but I am afraid that I will not be able to come.

3. First of all, allow me to extend a warm welcome to our guests _____ (代表到场的全体人员).

4. _____ (我不得不向你投诉) the quality of the goods that you recently sent us.

5. _____ (我想借此机会) to express my gratitude for your help.

6. _____ (我的推荐人会告诉您) that I can fulfill the particular requirements of your bookkeeping position.

Report Practice

TEMPLATE

Headline: give the main _____ of the ad

Body: introduce the _____ or _____,

   explain the _____,

   ask for an action

Slogan: create a corporate _____

Practice 7

Compose a commercial advertisement with the given information according to the template above.

A. one-week money back guarantee

B. the new product is right before your eyes

C. specializes in manufacturing cell phones

D. Communication unlimited

E. good quality and portable size

F. in order to meet users' demand for a multi-functional cell phone

---

Motorola Cell Phone

Motorola Inc. is a company that (1) _____ . Motorola has come out with many models of the Droid. Several months ago, (2) _____ , a group of company experts began a new research project. Now, (3) _____ . With its multi-functions, it can be used as a calculator, a computer, an alarm clock, a game player, a message sender among other uses. It features a pleasing design, (4) _____ . Services offered:

a one-year warranty

(5) _____

free delivery

(6) _____ .

Manufacturer: Motorola, Inc.

Tel.: 027-56248888

Address: 50#Huanghe Rd, Wuhan, China

Website: http://www.motorola.com

Practice 8

Read the information below and complete the commercial advertisement, adding details where necessary.

Imagine Apollo wants to place an ad for their fashions to be sold at a reduced price. It is a galaxy of spring fashions. They offer a sales fair to show kinds of traditional garments, fur coats, top quality sweaters, down garments, children's clothes, cowboy suits, etc. Fashion shows will be given every Saturday and Sunday from December 25, 2011 to January 3, 2012.

Loudi Apollo Shopping Centre
Spring Fashion Sales Fair

Time: (1) _____

Place: (2) _____

Articles on display: (3) _____, etc.

(4) _____ will be given by professional models from Loudi Apollo Commercial Group
at 10:00 —11:00 am, 3:00 —4:00 pm every (5) _____.

(6) _____ at Loudi Apollo Shopping Centre.

All are welcome.

🍀 Practice 9

Complete the following advertisement according to the Chinese information given below.

PEARLS and JEWELRY by CHOW TAI FOOK

(1) _____(驰名商标) of China Rich varieties

(2) _____(款式新颖) of classic & creative designs

(3) _____(优质的售后服务)

To be highly praised and appreciated by the consuming public.

(4) _____(价格合理) to every customer

Good reputation over the world, (5) _____(欢迎选购).

The Diamond is Forever! (钻石恒永远, 一颗永流传!)

Open every day 9:00 am—8:00 pm

Chow Tai Fook Jewelry Co., Ltd. (周大福珠宝金行有限公司)

Tel.: 400-166-9999

Website: http://www.ctf.com.cn/

Part IV
Supplementary Reading

Reading One

Sunlight Curtains!

Sunlight Curtains are new products of Mingyubuyi Curtain Co. Ltd. Made from specially imported cotton, the curtains will keep the light out in summer and prevent heat loss in winter. It also allows your furniture to be safe from the effects of fading and increases your privacy (私人空间).

Designed for easy care, the curtains are light in weigh and machine washable. They are easy to install on standard curtain rods (窗帘架) of your kitchens, bathrooms and bedrooms. The cover of these curtains has a stylish dragon print that gives your room a custom-decorated look.

We have various types and sizes available. Delivery can be made right from stock (现货供应). Available colors are: white, blue, pink, green and silver.

Services offered:

—one-week money back guarantee

—free delivery and installment

For more information, please call 244-676-8501.

Manufacturer: Mingyubuyi Curtain Co., Ltd.

Reading Two

Short-term Courses

To meet the needs for job, and knowledge of people from all walks of life, the Wald Education Group Co. Ltd. offers various short-term programs of courses which include English, Japanese, and computers.

These courses can be organized from two weeks to three months according to the interests and needs of groups numbering not fewer than 10. The date of application is the middle of January for spring short-term courses and the end of June for summer short-term courses.

The application fee is US$10 per person per course. The costs will vary according to the actual expenses of different courses.

Any individual or organization interested in any of these courses can contact Miss Liu Ying, Dean of Admissions at 021-6467-4778.

Select the Wald, select success!

The Wald Education Group Co. Ltd.

主要参考书目

[1] 晨梅梅.《实用写作教程》[M].上海：上海外语教育出版社，2006.

[2] 丁往道.《英语写作基础教程》[M].北京：高等教育出版社，2005.

[3]《高等学校应用能力考试过关丛书》编写组.《技能训练模拟试题》[M].长沙：湖南大学出版社，2001.

[4] 何维湘.《商务英语应用文写作》[M].广州：中山大学出版社，1997.

[5] 胡朝慧.《英语写作》[M].武汉：武汉理工大学出版社，2009.

[6] 胡英坤，车丽娟.《商务英语写作》[M].北京：外语教学与研究出版社，2005.

[7] 胡文仲.《实用英语写作》[M].北京：外语教学与研究出版社，1997.

[8] 黄瑛瑛.《世纪英语应用英语写作》[M].大连：大连理工大学出版社，2008.

[9] 蒋刻.《新职业英语》[M].北京：外语教学与研究出版社，2009.

[10] 考试命题研究小组.《历届真题实训（A 级）》[M].天津：天津大学出版社，2010.

[11] 李美，习会耀.《英语写作中级教程》[M].北京：高等教育出版社，2006.

[12] 李太志.《商务英语写作实训》[M].北京：国防工业出版社，2008.

[13] 潘琪，曹硕.《商务英语写作》[M].北京：中国宇航出版社，2009.338-346.

[14] 任奎艳.《世纪商务英语写作训练》[M].大连：大连理工大学出版社，2007.

[15] 谭外元，杨文地.《英文写作新编》[M].北京：机械工业出版社，2004.

[16] 王晓红.《经贸英语》[M].北京：外语教学与研究出版社，2009.

[17] 新编实用英语教材编写组.《新编实用英语》第二版 [M].北京：高等教育出版社，2007.

[18] 徐小贞.《商务英语写作》[M].北京：外语教学与研究出版社，2010.

[19] 虞苏美，张春柏.《新编商务英语写作1》[M].北京：高等教育出版社，2009.

[20] 张燕如.《应用英语写作》[M].北京：外语教学与研究出版社，2007.

[21] 朱巧莲.《商务英语写作实战案例》[M].北京：人民教育出版社，2010.38-53.

参考网址

http://www. asqql. com/html_file/427/263_1. html?jdfwkey=18auj2

http://www. assabsteels. com

http://www. bestsampleresume. com/letters/congratulation-letter-sample. html

http://writing. colostate. edu

http://www. diandian. net

http://www. eduzhai. net/zhichang/45/zhiye_6455. html

http://www2. elc. polyu. edu. hk/cill/eiw/memos. htm +改写

http://www. enmajor. com/cn/Html/Industy_English/BEC/6014994425410. html

http://www. enmajor. com/cn/Html/Industy_English/BEC/94824. html

http://www. exam8. com/english/BEC/gaoji/xiezuo/201105/2002677. html

http://www. fish4. co. uk

http://www. for68. com/new/2006/7/sw0986193653203760027800-0. htm

http://www. google. com. hk/search?q=career+vacancy&hl

http://www. google. com/imghp?hl=en&tab=wi

http://www. lsgskgchefs. com

http://www. wenku. baidu. com

http:// www. yourdictionary. com

http://www. youshang. com/content/2011/09/14/125162. html

http://theletterheads. net/category/congratulation-letter/

http://zhidao. baidu. com/question/238697387. html

http://www. 233. com/bec/zhongji/Write/20061102/164606406. html

http://www. 9998. tv/news/24907. html

中国人民大学出版社外语出版分社读者信息反馈表

尊敬的读者：

感谢您购买和使用中国人民大学出版社外语出版分社的 ＿＿＿＿＿＿＿＿＿ 一书，我们希望通过这张小小的反馈卡来获得您更多的建议和意见，以改进我们的工作，加强我们双方的沟通和联系。我们期待着能为更多的读者提供更多的好书。

请您填妥下表后，寄回或传真回复我们，对您的支持我们不胜感激！

1. 您是从何种途径得知本书的：
   □书店　　　　□网上　　　　□报纸杂志　　　　　□朋友推荐

2. 您为什么决定购买本书：
   □工作需要　　□学习参考　　□对本书主题感兴趣　　□随便翻翻

3. 您对本书内容的评价是：
   □很好　　　　□好　　　　□一般　　　　　□差　　　　□很差

4. 您在阅读本书的过程中有没有发现明显的专业及编校错误，如果有，它们是：
   ＿＿＿＿＿＿＿＿＿＿＿＿＿＿＿＿＿＿＿＿＿＿＿＿＿＿＿＿＿＿＿＿＿＿＿＿＿＿
   ＿＿＿＿＿＿＿＿＿＿＿＿＿＿＿＿＿＿＿＿＿＿＿＿＿＿＿＿＿＿＿＿＿＿＿＿＿＿
   ＿＿＿＿＿＿＿＿＿＿＿＿＿＿＿＿＿＿＿＿＿＿＿＿＿＿＿＿＿＿＿＿＿＿＿＿＿＿

5. 您对哪些专业的图书信息比较感兴趣：
   ＿＿＿＿＿＿＿＿＿＿＿＿＿＿＿＿＿＿＿＿＿＿＿＿＿＿＿＿＿＿＿＿＿＿＿＿＿＿
   ＿＿＿＿＿＿＿＿＿＿＿＿＿＿＿＿＿＿＿＿＿＿＿＿＿＿＿＿＿＿＿＿＿＿＿＿＿＿
   ＿＿＿＿＿＿＿＿＿＿＿＿＿＿＿＿＿＿＿＿＿＿＿＿＿＿＿＿＿＿＿＿＿＿＿＿＿＿

6. 如果方便，请提供您的个人信息，以便于我们和您联系（您的个人资料我们将严格保密）：
   您供职的单位：＿＿＿＿＿＿＿＿＿＿＿＿＿＿＿＿＿＿＿＿＿＿＿＿＿＿＿
   您教授的课程（教师填写）：＿＿＿＿＿＿＿＿＿＿＿＿＿＿＿＿＿＿＿＿＿
   您的通信地址：＿＿＿＿＿＿＿＿＿＿＿＿＿＿＿＿＿＿＿＿＿＿＿＿＿＿＿
   您的电子邮箱：＿＿＿＿＿＿＿＿＿＿＿＿＿＿＿＿＿＿＿＿＿＿＿＿＿＿＿

请联系我们：黄婷　程子殊　于真妮　商希建　鞠方安

电话：010-62512737，62513265，62515037，62514974，62515576

传真：010-62514961

E-mail：huangt@crup.com.cn　　chengzsh@crup.com.cn　　yuzn@crup.com.cn
　　　　shandysxj@163.com　　jufa@crup.com.cn

通信地址：北京市海淀区中关村大街甲 59 号文化大厦 15 层　　邮编：100872

中国人民大学出版社外语出版分社